THE MYSTERY OF GOD'S MERCY

STORIES AND MEDITATIONS

GEORGE T. MONTAGUE, SM

Paulist Press
New York / Mahwah, NJ

Cover design by Joe Gallagher
Book design by Lynn Else

Library of Congress Cataloging-in-Publication Data
Names: Montague, George T., author.
Title: The mystery of God's mercy : stories and meditations / George T. Montague, SM.
Description: New York / Mahwah, NJ : Paulist Press, [2022] | Summary: "This inspirational book is about finding God in the lives of those who live the Word of God"—Provided by publisher.
Identifiers: LCCN 2022000051 (print) | LCCN 2022000052 (ebook) | ISBN 9780809156047 (paperback) | ISBN 9780809187638 (ebook)
Subjects: LCSH: Word of God (Christian theology)—Miscellanea. | God (Christianity)—Mercy—Miscellanea. | Christian life—Anecdotes.
Classification: LCC BT180.W67 M66 2022 (print) | LCC BT180.W67 (ebook) | DDC 220.1/3—dc23/eng/20220525
LC record available at https://lccn.loc.gov/2022000051
LC ebook record available at https://lccn.loc.gov/2022000052

ISBN 978-0-8091-5604-7 (paperback)
ISBN 978-0-8091-8763-8 (e-book)

Published by Paulist Press
997 Macarthur Boulevard
Mahwah, New Jersey 07430
www.paulistpress.com

Printed and bound in the
United States of America

Among the many who formed me in my youth, I salute:
my early mentor, John Marvin Hunter,
publisher of the Frontier Times *and founder of*
the Frontier Times Museum,
who published my monthly tabloid newspaper from
ages 11 to 15 in Bandera, Texas,
and
Marianist Brother Roy Cherrier, who tutored me in
literature and creative writing at
Central Catholic High School
in San Antonio, Texas.

CONTENTS

PREFACE

Something amazing happens in the parable of the sower and the seed (Mark 4:1–9; Matt 13:1–13; Luke 8:4–10). The seed, Jesus says, is the Word of God. But then he goes on to say, "Those who are sown...." He then gives the types of soil in which the seed is sown, some on the path, others on rocky ground, others among thorns, and others on rich soil. The results differ drastically. But did you notice the shift in this parable? Did you notice the shift in the meaning of the seed? First, the seed is the Word of God; but when sown, it becomes people.

In other words, we can find the Word of God, the living Word, in the lives of those who live the Word. If you ask a Christian where they can find the Word of God, they are likely to say, "In the Bible." But the words in the Bible are only a unique combination of printer's ink and paper. The Word does not live there. It lives only when it is brought to life in a living subject, in a human person. And that is not just when a person reads it or repeats it, but when that person lives it. Thus, we can see the gospel come alive in the faith experiences of our fellow believers, and our own faith can be built up by their testimonies. If you want to understand Jesus's words "I was hungry and you gave me food, I was thirsty and you gave me something to drink..." (Matt

25:35–46), read the life of Mother Teresa of Kolkata. The lives of the saints are the footnotes of the gospel.

That is why, in teaching the New Testament to college students over the years, I have asked them to write a story from their own life illustrating how they experienced a word of the gospel. For the same reason, I have found that sharing my own struggle to live the gospel has been life-giving to many people.

Jesus taught with stories. And so have I at high school, college, and graduate school levels, and, of course, through homilies and talks at conferences. I have no idea how much my listeners retain of what I have taught, but I do know that what they remember most are the stories I have shared. That is why, when my provincial suggested that I write a book on mercy, I knew that I had no taste for a theological treatise on the subject. But I did have a lifetime of stories—my own experiences of God's mercy and the experiences of others.

This book tells stories of God's mercy in my life and the lives of friends and students who have given permission for them to be shared. Some of my stories are meditations on the stories of mercy in the Bible seen through the eyes of those who told them or those who wrote them.

Mercy can mean many things. It can mean giving mercy, as when we do an act of kindness. It can mean receiving mercy, as when someone forgives us, and especially when God forgives us. It can mean the heroic gift of self to save someone's life. Mercy is one of the names of God. The stories that follow show the many facets of mercy.

All of us are on a journey. Hearing the stories of fellow travelers will often evoke our own. My hope is that the ones I share here will do just that for you.

1

———————

MERCY IS
MYSTERY

When I began writing this book, the sun was rising on my eighty-sixth year. People confirm what my doctor has already stated, that I am in astonishingly good health for my age. When I ask them to guess my age, they usually fall ten or fifteen years short of target. I have been blessed, abundantly. And yet, shocking memories crowd my thoughts: my beautiful niece, Regina, thrown from her car and smashed to death by an eighteen-wheeler at the age of twenty-five; Ana, a victim of cancer at sweet sixteen, buried in a white coffin covered with permanent markers scrolling farewells by teenage friends; my brother, Charlie, killed at the age of twenty-one on a beach in the South Pacific by a rain of Japanese bullets. How does one make sense of all this inequality? Why eighty-six instead of six? Why am I here and they are not?

Maybe I'm feeling guilty—however twisted it may be—like the guilt a soldier feels when his buddy alongside him is killed. Survivor guilt: Why him and not me? Is there a God in all of this or is it just fate?— the first questions that came to my father as he grasped the Marine telegram that read, "Deeply regret to inform you...."

If I am to speak of mercy, I need to face the question posed by the name of the order of sisters who taught me in grade school: the Sisters of Divine Providence. Providence? Divine Providence? Does so much inequality in humanity speak of providence? Or is it chaos or chance or...was my father's first intuition right: fate?

The mystery remains for me as it does for many, but there are other voices that offer a palliative to these turbulent questions. Out of millennia past comes one who has wrestled with suffering because he has endured it: Job. In the preface to the Book of Job's thirty-five chapters, where Job struggles with the mystery of inequality while pelted by "friends" who assured him that they knew the answers, the iconic sufferer says, "The LORD gave, and the LORD has taken away; blessed be the name of the LORD" (Job 1:21). It is the answer at which he will arrive after rejecting the claims of his accusers and encountering the Lord instead. But the Lord does not come to him with tight-fit answers. Instead, the Lord comes to him in a storm and pelts him with questions of his own. But God's storm dispels the storm of debate. In the storm, Job meets God. Thereafter, Job will walk by faith rather than by sight. But that satisfies because God knows when Job doesn't. And that's okay with Job because he has met the Lord in a personal experience of faith.

But Job does know one thing: "The LORD *gave*...." It was all gift in the first place. This could have been a conclusion of reason, but often it requires faith to see it. Indeed, life is a gift, but like every gift, the receiver has no right to say, "Why not more?" It was the same question the vineyard workers asked when they saw that the latecomers were paid as much as those who arrived early. There is no injustice in God giving more gifts to some than he gives to others. He is the giver and judge of the measure. We are neither giver nor judge. We are the undeserving gifted.

That is why I have learned to hold everything— every gift and every breath—with a light and grateful grasp. Light because I know not how long it will last; grateful because it is a gift, a total gift, and it tells of a Giver, whom I have come to know. Like the flower, the gifts may fade, but the Giver never will.

But what about the journey? If life is a gift, why is there a mixture of gift and grief in the living of it? Why is it more painful for some than for others? And why are some born with disabilities? Here, too, facile answers will not do. We live in a cloud of unknowing. I cannot, nor would I dare to, reason about evil, as Augustine does in his book *On Evil*, when I face the redheaded teenager dying before me with an aggressive cancer. The only answer is the one I have in my hand—a crucifix. Suffering and death are part of the story. But only a part. Faith will turn the page to see the final chapter, where the victim is the victor.

If life itself, long or short, is a gift, is there a Provident Hand in the events that mark our journey? The unbeliever cannot see it. On the one hand, unlike Beethoven, who, legend says, on his deathbed in a thunderstorm raised his fist in defiance at the Almighty, the unbeliever has no fist to raise to the void. If life is meaningless, so is death. On the other hand, the believer's rearview mirror reveals blessings that have lit his past—even the bumps and turns have etched a plan—and made a story of the dance between his free hand and the hand of God. He may at times have let go of the stronger hand (moves that he sorrows for now), but even more joyful was the rescuing embrace. The tapestry of our life may look rough and unkempt, but that is only because we are looking at the back side, waiting to see what the Weaver sees on the front.

Sometimes the Weaver startles us by finishing his masterpiece early—too early for our comfort, as with Regina. And sometimes we wonder why he is taking so long, as with me. That's part of the mystery.

After I had written that the key is that life is a gift, I became a close friend with a farmer who offered his own wisdom. Cliff's wisdom was etched by soil and plow—and pain. His young wife, Dawn, had died of cancer, leaving his twin daughters motherless at age seven. Then the death of three family members in seven days pushed him over the cliff (no pun intended). He sank into what doctors call a reactive depression. Word was that he had rejected the faith, the church, and even God. I was worried when my call was not returned. I left a message of love, support, and prayer. Finally, he called and came to see me. Healing was happening. In the long conversation, one thing he said, concerning the loved ones he had just lost, was "God is a farmer. He picks the fruit when it is ripe."

2

MERCY IN
THE HEBREW
SCRIPTURES

In the Beginning
There Was Mercy

When I open the front door to get the morning paper, I see that the symphony of stars to which I said goodnight has given way to a burnt-orange dawn in the east. I breathe in the morning air and praise God for the beauty that wraps me in a robe of joy. Back in the dining room, I open the paper and see blood—war, crime, rape, hatred—the fingerprint of evil. The good news of creation yields to the bad news of humanity.

New readers of the first eleven chapters of Genesis often find them a confusing jumble of stories and genealogies. But with guidance and insight, one can discover that they present a powerful response to the question raised by the contrast of my morning sequence. It is a question that every thinking human ultimately asks: On the one hand, why is there so much order, beauty, and harmony—in short, goodness—in the world and, on the other hand, so much chaos, ugliness, discord—in short, evil—in the world? Welcome to the prelude to the cosmic story of God's mercy.

There are, in fact, two stories of Creation in Genesis: the first telling us of the goodness of creation; the second, how it became corrupted by evil. In the first story, there is a constant refrain after each day of Creation: "And God saw that it was good" (Gen 1:10). And when he crowned his work with man and woman, he saw that "indeed, it was very good" (Gen 1:31).

Then we have the second story of Creation told from a different viewpoint. The first story begins with a watery chaos and ends up with dry land. The second story begins with a desert and ends up with enough water for God to gather mud to shape man as would a potter and then breathe into this creature the breath of life and behold: Adam. Then God creates the animals and brings them one by one to the man, but after the long procession, Adam is not satisfied. He is lonely. So, God takes a rib from his side and gives him a bride, and he shouts that now he has a companion that is an equal: "This at last is bone of my bones and flesh of my flesh" (Gen 2:23). God places them both in a garden of delights, where their greatest joy is their friendship with their maker. He takes a walk with them every afternoon. They are innocent and loving. Everything is beautiful, everything is in order in the outward world and in their inward world.

But there is a snake, a talking snake, in the garden, and he invites Eve to taste of the tree of which God told them not to eat. He sows the seed of distrust: the tree is the secret of God's own knowledge, and God doesn't want her to have it. And Eve, noticing first the beauty of the fruit, its probable delicious taste, and then, as the snake said, seeing it as the door to knowing all that God knows, she takes the fruit. Notice that she did not consult her husband before making the decision. She eats it and hands it to her husband who, without questioning, eats it. They both then realize that the fruit is spiritual poison.

All hell breaks loose. Their nakedness now becomes a source of shame; they pass the blame: "The woman whom you gave to be with me, she gave me fruit from the tree, and I ate" (Gen 3:12); "The serpent tricked me, and I ate" (Gen 3:13). Even nature rebels with thorns and thistles; work is drudgery and childbearing painful; and most of all, the heart of the tragedy—their disobedience—breaks the bond of friendship with their Creator. Theologically, the first couple is estranged from God, from self, from others, and from nature. They must leave the garden.

But here God first reveals his mercy: God clothes their nakedness from the coldness of the world they have chosen through their sin. Moreover, he announces warfare with the serpent whom we now know is Satan, but a war in which the seed of the woman will win out over the evil one. It was a risk God took in giving the king and queen of creation free will. God wanted a creature who could respond to his love in a way that the rocks, the birds, and the squirrels could not, namely, a conscious communion of love. We could call that God's plan A. But he was ready with a plan B in case they messed up. It would be a more painful path, but God's plan to save would not be defeated by humanity's rebellion. If there was "mercy" in plan A, there was "Mercy" with a capital M in plan B—a Mercy that would ultimately be nailed to a cross.

But we are getting ahead of the story. The sin of Adam and Eve releases a landslide of evil. Not only a passing of blame, but murder, as Cain kills his brother Abel. Then Lamech, who now has two wives, tells them that, while hunting, he killed a boy who happened to wound him and that, henceforth, Lamech will take seventy-times revenge on anyone who merely hurts him. And so, we witness the escalation of revenge. It is no longer just an eye for an eye and a tooth for a tooth, but if you hurt one of my people, I will kill two and more of yours. It is a scene we still see today in tribal warfare—unlimited revenge.

God's mercy intervenes to save Noah from the flood that cleanses the world of evil. But that act of mercy is soon thwarted by the sin of Noah's descendants. Despite the rise of skills and industry, humanity gets in such a mess by its own pride—the building of a tower that will reach the heavens—that they can no longer communicate with each other. They no longer talk the same language. Now alienated from each other, they disperse into the world that they will have to tame, one group not caring for another. Do you hear the drums of tribal warfare, even genocide in the distance— the gas chambers in Auschwitz, the rivers of blood in Rwanda?

Chapter 11 of Genesis challenges the reader to ask, Is there any hope for humanity? Must the mercy of God always be thwarted? God answers, My mercy will not be defeated. It may take a long time, but my mercy will win out. I will start with one man. We turn the page and meet Abraham.

Waiting for Mercy

It was not the climate that choked him in Ur but the gods and goddesses that lined every path in the old town. There was something in him that longed for greater simplicity, for the fresh air of shepherding that disposed him to hear an inner voice telling him to move on. That would become his vocation—to be on the move, to spend his life as a pilgrim, never settling long anywhere. It was not unlike today's military families. This was Abram, soon to be named Abraham, father of a people. And so, he left Ur, moved to Haran, and on to Canaan, surveying the land where, in a distant future, his descendants—as numerous as the stars or the sands of the seashore, the Voice promised—would eventually dwell. Could he, a man in his mid-seventies with no son or daughter to give evidence to the promise, believe it? This mysterious, shapeless God, who had only a voice and a promise, was so compelling when he spoke that Abraham obeyed without question.

But the hardest thing was to continue to believe as the shadows of his life and Sarah's lengthened, and the only pledge of the promise was that day when God sent a flaming oven between the animal halves and swore a covenant to the patriarch, without demanding that he walk through the halves as any covenant-making in those days would demand. No, this was all promise on the part of the Voice…but where was the son? Still, Abraham believed.

He often asked the Lord, "Why?" Why must I wait so long, even to an impossible age for you to do what you promised? Did he realize that waiting for mercy is mercy itself if it draws one closer to Mercy? Did he realize that, into distant millennia, mothers like Monica would follow his path as she waited in prayer for Augustine to find the Beauty ever ancient, ever new? When at last a baby boy's cry rang through Abraham's tent, he forgot the decades of waiting for the joy that God had vowed. God had shown his mercy. The old man's trembling hands held the promise.

But not for long. Isaac was hardly bar-mitzvah age when the Lord told the elderly parent to take him to Mount Moriah and sacrifice him. Abraham obeyed but, in the long journey, questions tortured him. God, why do you make a promise and then command the opposite? Are you the kind of God who is no different from the Canaanites of this land, who throw their first born into the fire thinking it pleases you? I thought you were a God of mercy, not a God who consumes the very people you create. They walked on, the father carrying knife and fire and, at his side young, wood-bearing Isaac who finally asked the obvious: "Father… the fire and the wood are here, but where is the lamb for a burnt offering?" (Gen 22:7). The old man waited till God gave him a word that would say more than the truth he spoke: "God himself will provide the lamb for a burnt offering, my son" (Gen 22:8).

On the surface, it got the father out of trouble; deeper down, it laid the responsibility on the Voice that seemed to erase the promise and worse. Why did you ever make the promise if you were going to have me kill my son who fulfilled it? Millennia later, there would be another son carrying wood up a mount. Abraham did not see it. He was suffering his own passion as he struggled up Moriah, the passion of compassion for his son. Millennia later there would also be a mother suffering the passion of compassion for her son bearing wood up a mount. Mary would immortalize Abraham in her Magnificat. Did she think of this scene as Jesus carried the wood and she the fire of a mother's love and the knife that pierced her heart?

At the last second, an invisible arm blocked Abraham's and the knife about to pierce the heart of his son. No, the Voice said, all I wanted to know is whether you thought of the boy or me as the assurance of posterity. He was, after all, gift, and you were willing to offer him back to me. That is all I wanted to know. You must never forget whose gift Isaac is. And there is something else I want you to know: neither you nor the people who will issue from you will ever have my permission to kill their offspring. I want my mercy to be written in every parent's heart. But I want them to hold their children with the relaxed grasp that knows from whom and for whom they received those gifts.

The story of Abraham is not a mere artifact. Through it, God speaks to humanity of every age, including ours. He wants children to be cherished, not abused. Father, when your anger raises your hand to strike, pray for an angel of mercy to stay your hand. If you are a mother, learn to correct without demeaning. Uncle, your niece's body is not yours to abuse; neither is a boy a toy for an elder's lust.

Abraham believed in the God of mercy. That's why, in his turn, he showed mercy where justice did not demand it: intercession. When the Lord told him the wickedness of Sodom had become so great that it was headed for destruction, Abraham interceded. Lord, will you destroy the just along with the wicked? What if there are fifty righteous people in the city? The Lord responds that he will not destroy the city if there are fifty. Abraham realizes there may not be that many, so he bargains the Lord step by step down to ten. Abraham's heart of mercy leads him to intercede for the city.

The people of mercy are thus to intercede for mercy. In her apparitions, the daughter of Abraham urges his children and hers to storm heaven for the entire world—the Sodom of today. The threat of disaster may not be annihilation by an apocalyptic angel nor heaven-sent fire and brimstone, but the world's own self-destructive appetites. But as the prophetic Lady assures, the future can be fashioned by prayer. So teaches the Bible; so teaches the God of mercy.

The Cycle of Renewal (Psalm 51)

The earthen oil lamp could be cupped in his hand, but its tiny flame was enough to bare the troubled face of the Psalmist, whose wife and two children, blanketed in bed in the cramped home, had been asleep for an hour, while he lay awake. Exiled and not yet called by the captor king to serve in the royal scriptorium, he suffered even more than his fellow Jews from the loss of the temple, where sins could be atoned by sacrifice and where he had penned some of the finest psalms. But there was something more troubling. In a moment of anger and frustration, he had let slip a curse at his lot, blaming his God for it all. He had sinned. Gazing at the blank papyrus before him and dipping his feather pen in the inkwell he had slipped under his cloak as he was driven from the temple in Jerusalem, he began to scratch his confession.

Have mercy on me, O God.... Tears welled in his eyes, but he brushed them aside lest they moisten the papyrus. He looked at the two Hebrew words staring

15

back at him. No, he thought, I have no claim of my own for that mercy, and I am lost if I focus on the enormity of my sin. More enormous is your mercy than any sin. Your mercy is boundless. And so, he scratched further: ...*according to your abundant mercy*. I cannot merit mercy; it is all your gift. That is why demanding it in justice is out of the question; I can only beg you for it.

The Psalmist resumed writing what would become the second best-known psalm in the Old Testament, yielding only to the Shepherd Psalm. It would become Psalm 51, known in the Latin tradition as the *Miserere*.

Aware of the filth of his sin, the Psalmist asks his God to erase his offense, wash out his guilt, and cleanse him of his sin. He believes God can do this, and his need is extreme. He has no excuse to parade before God. *I know my transgressions, and my sin is ever before me*. It was not an offense against my neighbor. No. *Against you, you alone, have I sinned, and done what is evil in your sight*.

He pauses and recalls the time after a dispute at the city gates, when one of two men bowed his head and said, "You are right. I admit I was wrong." The Psalmist now bows his head before God. *You are justified in your sentence and blameless when you pass judgment*.

But then it occurs to him that he might have a claim on God's mercy, not because of any good work but precisely because, like every other human being, he has been a sinner since birth, even since his conception. *Indeed,* he writes, *I was born guilty, a sinner when my mother conceived me.* Maybe that might touch God's pity.

And then another thought strikes him. God loves truth. God is Truth. Admission of my sin, that I have offended him, is truth. Instead of concealing or making excuses for my sin, I have laid it out before him. *You desire truth in the inward being; therefore teach me wisdom in my secret heart.* So, the gift of truth opens the door to God's wisdom, to seeing things as God sees them. And how does God see them? As a chance to show his mercy.

The Psalmist considers how mercy can turn an ugly thing into something of beauty. *Wash me* [as only you can do], *and I shall be whiter than snow. Let me hear joy and gladness; let the bones that you have crushed rejoice.* He senses that the forgiveness he has begged is being given at this very moment, and the joy of a festival is beginning to refresh his soul.

But he wants more than forgiveness and cleansing. He doesn't want to fall again. *So, I ask for a steadfast, faithful, persevering spirit. In fact, it's the gift of your own holy Spirit I need that holy breath of yours that assures me your face is close to mine. O do that, Lord, and be my permanent respirator.*

He writes faster. *Then I will sing your praise. I will tell others of your mercy, and sinners like me will return to you.* Yes, to *You,* because that is true repentance and renewal. *It's not about the blood and smoke of sacrifices.*

Yes, we had the temple, and blood and smoke spoke of our desire to please you. But now I know, as if I never knew before, that *a truly repentant heart is worth more than all the sacrifices in the world.* It's all about landing in your embrace once more, in being one with you in love.

The face once tortured with dark guilt beams now with its own light—peace, joy, and thanksgiving. The Psalmist has experienced the whole cycle of renewal—repentance, confession, renewal in the Holy Spirit, and sharing the good news of God's mercy with others. On the papyrus lay the score of a song that would teach millions like you and me how to repent and revive.

3

GOD'S MERCY ENFLESHED

Zechariah and Mary were Jews who clung to centuries of hope for the hour of salvation, the coming of the Anointed One, the Messiah. Their voices were the first to proclaim in song that the time of fulfillment had come. Thinking less of their own honor than of the honor of their people, they sang of the Lord:

> His mercy is for those who fear him
>> from generation to generation....
> By the tender mercy of our God,
>> the dawn from on high will break upon us,
> to give light to those who sit in darkness and
>> in the shadow of death.
>> (Luke 1:50, 78–79)

The birth of Mary's child fulfilled those promises in the flesh.

irty years later, when Jesus emerged from the urity of a carpenter's workshop and walked up to e podium, unrolled the Scripture, and proclaimed that the Spirit of the Lord had anointed him, it was not for a mission of conquest but for a mission of mercy— the good news to the poor, liberty to captives, sight for the blind, and freedom for the oppressed. Pages of the New Testament detail the accomplishment of that program. It was also launching a program that would continue in the healing ministry of his disciples during and beyond his earthly life. Hospitals, schools, missions of mercy would soon emerge in a world sown with self-interest. Most importantly, if the world wanted peace it would have to embrace justice, reconciliation, and forgiveness born of love. For that, he was willing to die on a cross embossed with his blood, saying, "Father, forgive them; for they do not know what they are doing" (Luke 23:34).

Jesus was not only the giver of mercy; he was the receiver of mercy. He would allow a sinful woman to bathe his feet with her tears, another to anoint his head with precious oil, and Martha and other women to feed him, to say nothing of the nourishment and care given him by Mary and Joseph as he grew up.

This is an important lesson for those who think that they must always be serving, always giving, and never receiving. Sometimes the best gift we can give is to receive another's gift. It acknowledges their love and generosity and encourages them.

When we were children, we were eager to receive the gift, tore it open vigorously, gloated over it with little regard to the giver. I am reminded of a home Mass I said for my family, during which I invited the youngest child, Rachel, to help me in giving the homily. Rachel was four, shy, but finally she was coaxed into being my visual and audial aid.

It was Christmas, so my first question was this: "Rachel, what is Christmas all about?"

There was no answer. Perhaps the question was too theological. So, I tried again. "Are we celebrating the birthday of Jesus?"

A nod was all I got.

"And do we give gifts?" This got a more vigorous nod.

"And what do you do when you get a gift?" Coaching whispers wafted from the adults around the room: "You say thanks. You say thanks."

But Rachel would hear none of it. She looked at me as if I just asked the most stupid question in the world.

"YOU OPEN IT!" she exclaimed.

We had to assure Rachel that far from giving the wrong answer, hers was surprisingly correct—for one her age. Hopefully in her later years, she will treasure the love of the giver more than the gift.

So too for us with the gifts of Jesus. There is certainly nothing more necessary for us than our salvation. But do we see and treasure the infinite love he has for us behind the gift? If we reflect on the brutal price that he did not *have* to pay, *but did so* to win our love, we will realize that what is most important is for us to be one with him in an eternal embrace of love.

Mercy Re-creates

Like hail dancing on a tin roof, the sounds of rock cutters chipping at building blocks for Herod's temple provided the audio for daily life in Jerusalem that day. But suddenly, the workers stopped to watch a crowd of Pharisees pushing a woman forward and shouting, "Adulterer!" Were they going to stone her? Maybe, but that was not their primary intention. They were going to use her for their purposes. Jesus was in the temple area, and that is where they stopped. They would test the prophet from Galilee who was claiming to be the new Moses, daring to revise the Torah.

"Moses said we should stone her," they fired the question, fully aware that there were plenty of stones at hand. "What do you say?"

Jesus turned an ear of disinterest and began writing on the ground. There is no record of what he wrote, if indeed it was anything more than doodling, the kind of thing we do when what we are hearing is of no interest to us. Some scholars think he was fulfilling Jeremiah: "Those who turn away from you will be written in the dust" (Jer 17:13 NIV). But since the author of the story did not think what Jesus wrote was worth recording, it seems that the best understanding is that Jesus was just doodling, showing complete lack of interest. Annoyed, they pressed the question again and again. Jesus finally straightened up and said, "Let anyone among you who is without sin be the first to throw a stone at her" (John 8:7).

Nonplussed, and aware of the Psalm, "For no one living is righteous before you" (Ps 143:2), they peel off one by one and leave the woman alone with Jesus.

"Where are they?" Jesus asks, "Has no one condemned you?

"No one, sir."

What is she thinking? Glad, no doubt, to be rescued from her accusers, she trembles under her self-image created by the men she has known. She is either their tool for pleasure or the butt of their condemnation. Even now, she has been used as a tool for their plot. Either way, she is trash; she has no future.

But Jesus sees gold where others see trash. "Neither do I condemn you." It is the second moment of unbinding: not only is she physically free from her accusers but freed from the sentence Jesus might have given. She hears the word of mercy for the first time.

Whatever happened to that woman? If the gospel writers thought her story worth telling, then they probably knew that she gladly fulfilled Jesus's words, "Go your way, and from now on do not sin again" (John 8:11), and became a member of the new community gathered around Jesus during his ministry and after the resurrection. Like Mary Magdalen, she embodied the triumph of grace over evil. Indeed, many are the stories of those whose lives, once deemed trash even by themselves, have been gilded by the Master metallurgist to be the gold of the kingdom. Meeting Jesus, the divine squanderer of mercy, made the difference.

Monica had been a woman like that. She had lived in moral filth, including a stint as a stripteaser, until she met Jesus in a Christian community where she discovered the beauty of real love and so discovered her real self, her beautiful self, made so by Jesus.

Jim had used women for sex and paid for four abortions. In a moment of awakening, he wept copiously. His tears of repentance put him on a road of healing.

Mercy is more than forgiveness of sin. It begins a process of healing the self-inflicted wounds caused by sin. Just as a hospital patient needs time and attention to recover from a serious operation, so, too, do those recovering from a life dominated by sin. They need the nourishment of the sacraments, the healing power of the Word, and the love and warmth of a community of believers who themselves, having found Jesus, are going through the healing process. That is why small faith-sharing groups are so important as a substructure of a parish. Finally, the recovering sinner needs the gift of the Holy Spirit. It is not sufficient to drive out the evil spirits through renouncing the old life. Jesus warns that an empty house invites squatters. The patient needs the infilling of the Holy Spirit.

Crashing the Party

Jesus is a giver. He gives his word when he teaches. He gives his peace when he heals. He gives his joy when he raises the dead. Most of all, he gives his own life on the cross—and in the bread and the cup of the Eucharist.

But Jesus is also a receiver. Giving is not the only language of love. Sometimes the greatest gift we can give someone is to receive their love. In so doing, we honor their ability to love. Perhaps that is why Jesus never refused an invitation. If he teaches and evangelizes by his healings, he also teaches and evangelizes by saying yes when another human heart breathes welcome.

One such moment (Luke 7:36–50) happened when a servant caught up with Jesus and said, "My master would be pleased if you would dine with him and his friends tonight."

"And who is your master?" Jesus replied.

"He is Simon the Pharisee."

Jesus raised his eyebrows. "Simon the Pharisee?" What was surprising about this invitation was its source: a Pharisee, one of those with whom Jesus often locked horns. Here was an opportunity not given Jesus when he argued with the Pharisees in the public forum. On the one hand, to share one's table was to share intimacy and friendship. Perhaps Simon's heart had really been touched by Jesus's preaching. Perhaps, like Nicodemus, he already believed in his heart. On the other

25

hand, it could be a trap. Perhaps Simon had invited his Pharisee friends to provide a forum for trapping Jesus. Brushing aside his disciples' mistrust and even his own, Jesus accepted the invitation.

What was in Simon's mind when he dared to do what no other Pharisee had dared to do: invite the "prophet" of Galilee to dinner? Whatever was in his mind, Simon treated Jesus with the caution of a circus trainer facing a new tiger. He welcomed Jesus into his home without washing the feet of his guest or embracing him with shalom. Simon was torn by his Pharisaic flight from the common and the filthy, on the one hand, and by his heart, on the other. Invite this "prophet," but be careful; other Pharisees are watching.

The Pharisee's servants still have in their hands the herbs to start the meal when a woman from the street crashes the party, runs, and falls at the feet of Jesus. The servants freeze. Simon's jaw drops, speechless. He would normally have ordered the servants to hustle her back to the street were it not for the smile of Jesus welcoming the woman. It takes but a moment for Simon to realize that this prostitute is not trying to seduce Jesus, for she is weeping. Tears flood rills graven by profligate years, but they flow from eyes knowing the joy of being forgiven, for Jesus had just met her in the street and, upon her kneeling sorrow, forgiven her. They are tears of repentance but also tears of joy. As the tears abate, she grasps the hair that had seduced so many, and dries the feet of Jesus. Then she opens a vase of costly oil and anoints the feet she has kissed. A mystic would see a prophecy of the day when billions, upon repentance, would be washed and anointed, given new life in the sacraments.

Simon's shock turns to anger, "If this man were a prophet, he would know who and what sort of woman is touching him—that she is a sinner." He doesn't say this aloud, but in his flushed face, Jesus reads Simon's thoughts. What pierced the Pharisee's gut was her *touch*, for that kind of intimacy, touching the unclean, or being touched by them, was precisely what every Pharisee abhorred.

Jesus does not condemn his host any more than he does the woman. He gently invites a listening heart. "Simon, I have something to say to you."

"Tell me, teacher," Simon says, willing to hear the rabbi's words. What is the tone of his voice? Is it sarcastic? Or is he really seeking enlightenment? Luke, the narrator, lets us guess.

Then Jesus tells the story of two debtors, one owing five hundred days' wages, the other, fifty. When the creditor forgives them both, which will love him more? Simon replies, "The one with the bigger debt."

Simon is hooked. Jesus has only to draw the conclusion: the contrast between Simon and the woman. Unlike him, she has a broken heart, broken, first, by her unworthiness, but then by the unmerited, unspeakable gift of a love that forgives. It's not that her love has merited forgiveness. It's the other way around. Gifted by a forgiving love, she bursts forth in an extravagant drama of love: bathing tears, tender kisses, drying hair, costly ointment. It's as if Jesus's mercy has uncapped an artesian well that now floods the dining hall. There is another artesian well in the room—Simon's heart—but it is capped by a cold, distant, judgmental self-righteousness. If only he would admit it. If only he might let forgiving love uncap it.

Does Simon remain in his distance, or does he allow his heart to melt by Jesus's forgiving love? We don't know. Luke, the narrator, has left the story for each of us to finish. For there is in our heart an artesian well. Is it capped or clogged? Are we Simon, the trapped, or the woman set free?

4

ICONS
OF MERCY

I t's just an accident that Peter, Paul, and Mary, the famous singing trio of the 1960s, had the same names as three of the best-known converts of the New Testament. But the braiding witness of Jesus's three converts makes a harmony more beautiful and more lasting—two thousand years!—in a song of God's mercy. What good would the gift of his mercy be if there were no one to receive it? The three are Peter, the fisherman; Paul, the Apostle; and Mary Magdalen, the disciple. Separated in time, together they create a rich testimony to the God of mercy. We will consider each of them.

Peter

Suppose you were a fisherman two thousand years ago with no further horizon in life than the other side of the Sea of Galilee. Life was tough, especially if you did most of your fishing at nighttime. But life was simple. You knew how to fish, how to clean your nets, and how to read the weather, except for those storms that pounced upon the sea unannounced and turned it into a nauseating whirlpool. You could even manage them, provided you were not caught mid-sea in a boat that might capsize. Otherwise, you considered yourself fearless and secure. You are Peter.

But that changed the morning you were rowing back to shore after a fruitless night of fishing, bleary-eyed and musing on why your profession is called fishing rather than catching. You pulled ashore and began cleaning the nets of weeds, the only haul of the night. Further down the shore you spot a crowd moving toward you. Dropping your tools, you hear someone shout, "It's Jesus of Nazareth!" You have heard of him: a wonder-worker, a healer, a teacher. The crowd so presses on the famous figure, he is almost pushed into the water. You offer him your boat for a pulpit. Jesus teaches about forgiveness. Like several in the crowd, your face falls, remembering your grudge against your neighbor, Isaac, who borrowed your tackle a year ago and never returned it. You want to hear more, but Jesus turns to you and, with a grateful smile, says, "Put out for a catch."

"This is crazy," you think. "Master, we have worked all night long but have caught nothing. Yet if you say so, I will let down the nets" (Luke 5:5). The haul is so great you need help. You call your partners—

James and John—and fill their boat as well. You fall at Jesus's knees and cry, "Go away from me, Lord, for I am a sinful man!" (Luke 5:8). Jesus is no longer "Master"; he is *Lord*. You are given the grace to recognize the worker of the sign: Lord, the Son of the Living God. And in the presence of the All Holy, the contrast could not be greater: you are a sinner. Like Isaiah seeing a vision of the Lord in the temple and crying out, "Woe is me! I am lost, for I am a man of unclean lips...yet my eyes have seen the King, the LORD of hosts!" (Isa 6:5). You are seeing God, not in a vision, but in the flesh! You tremble with a fear you have never experienced before. All your securities are shaken, and you are overwhelmed by your unworthiness, your sinfulness.

If that revelation of Jesus was like an earthquake, Jesus's first words are another: "From now on you will be catching people"—both brush aside your cry for Jesus to leave you because you are a sinner. He calls you and your companions to be his full-time fishing team. No more is the other side of the lake your horizon. Your horizon is now the world. "There on the sand I have left my boat; at your side I will seek other seas." (*En la arena he dejado mi barca; junto a ti buscaré otro mar.*)

If you were asked how Peter is an icon of Jesus's mercy, you would probably think of Jesus's threefold pardon after the resurrection for Peter's threefold denial on the night of the passion. But have you noticed the similarity of these two scenes? Both happen at the same spot, the Sea of Galilee; and both crown unworthiness with commission: "You will be catching people" (Luke

5:10) in the first scene, and "Feed my sheep" (John 21:15–17) in the second. What is important, Jesus says, is not your weakness but my call. Where sin has abounded, my grace abounds even more.

What stands out here is not Peter's faith in Jesus but Jesus's faith in Peter. It is a faith that has no rational ground for success, certainly considering the second instance, when he publicly denied Jesus. Who could guarantee he would never do this again? Yet Jesus confides the whole church to his care.

This is a faith, a trust that creates. If you hire someone who has a brilliant resume, stellar recommendations, and an outstanding performance with a previous employer, you might say, "I'm sure I can trust her." But that is not trust. It is common sense. However, if you hire an ex-convict without proof of his performance, it takes an act of trust, an act of faith. And that act of trust can open a new and fruitful life for the convict. That is what Jesus does with Peter. There is great risk, as Jesus's trusting of Judas shows.

But Jesus's trust of Peter, in the face of his failure, creates a space for a new life, an explosion of generosity that will take him to Rome and ultimately to his own martyrdom. Jesus believes in Peter when Peter does not believe in himself.

So, we can imagine Peter's self-talk. "He believes in me! Believes in me after what I did! He believes in me, in what I still can be!" And then Peter remembers the night he walked on the waters. "When I looked at

the wind and waves instead of at Jesus, I sank. If I keep
my eyes on him, I can do the impossible."

And because of his own experience, he would tell
the whole world of the mercy of God. Jesus's trust in
Peter, despite the fisherman's failures, tells us we too
are called to use our gifts to spread the kingdom, not
because we are saints but despite our failures and sins.
Jesus has called you. He believes in you. Plead not your
weakness. Lean on his call.

Paul

A different drama of mercy comes onstage with
the Apostle Paul. He does not figure in the Gospels
like Peter. But he does figure prominently in the Acts
of the Apostles, and we have his own letters, including
what he says about his conversion and about mercy in
God's dealing with the Jews and the Gentiles in the
history of salvation. Let us begin with Paul's first letter to Timothy:

> I am grateful to Christ Jesus our Lord, who
> has strengthened me, because he judged me
> faithful and appointed me to his service,
> even though I was formerly a blasphemer,
> a persecutor, and a man of violence. But I
> received mercy because I had acted igno-
> rantly in unbelief, and the grace of our Lord
> overflowed for me with the faith and love

that are in Christ Jesus. The saying is sure and worthy of full acceptance, that Christ Jesus came into the world to save sinners—of whom I am the foremost. But for that very reason I received mercy, so that in me, as the foremost, Jesus Christ might display the utmost patience, making me an example to those who would come to believe in him for eternal life. (1 Tim 1:12–16)

Whether these words were written by Paul or by a later disciple—a matter of scholarly debate—they are the most extensive description of his conversion. They build on Paul's earlier references to his call by the risen Christ, especially the following: "Last of all, as to one untimely born, he appeared also to me. For I am the least of the apostles, unfit to be called an apostle, because I persecuted the church of God" (1 Cor 15:8–9); and "I was violently persecuting the church of God and was trying to destroy it" (Gal 1:13). Persecution of the church with the intention of destroying it—that is the only error, however serious, that he notes of his previous life. And he never says he sinned in doing so! He implies that he thought he was doing right in his zeal for the traditions of his fathers (see Gal 1:14). So, we wonder whether "blasphemer" and "arrogant man" in the letter to Timothy is faithful to Paul's assessment of himself in his earlier letters. The First Letter of Timothy goes on to diminish Paul's guilt by stating that he acted in ignorance. It is helpful here to distinguish between acts that are objectively sinful but subjectively innocent, as when we think we are doing right but later discover what we did was wrong. Paul's earlier letters describe his conversion not as turning from a life of immorality but as resulting from a divine *revelation* and a *mandate to mission*: "For I did not receive it from a human source, nor was I taught it, but I received it through a revelation of Jesus Christ" (Gal 1:12), and: "God, who had set me apart before I was born and called me through his grace, was pleased to reveal his Son to me, so that I might proclaim him among the Gentiles" (Gal 1:15–16). Here, Paul uses the language that the Lord uses when he calls and appoints Jeremiah as his prophet (see Jer 1:5). Like Jeremiah, Paul is thinking of his call not as a call from sin to repentance but as a call to be God's herald. As for his former life, Paul even says that what he did was out of zeal (see Gal 1:14; Phil 3:6).

Therefore, the major revelation of mercy in Paul's life was not primarily a moral conversion but an intellectual conversion and a call to mission. That, of course, was an act of divine mercy for the world—for you and me. In the history of the church there have been many such intellectual conversions: John Henry Newman, G. K. Chesterton, Jacques and Raissa Maritain, Edith Stein, to mention but a few.

Paul's *magna carta* on mercy is Romans 9—11. The Apostle spends three chapters dealing with what must have caused him much pain: If Christ is the fulfillment of the Old Testament, why have not the Jews as a people accepted him? Paul's answer: Though it seems that God's plan to save his people has failed because of their disbelief, what we see in the present time is that their failure has opened the gates of God's mercy to the Gentiles, to all non-Jews, to the whole world. Eventually, Paul prophesies, when the full number of the Gentiles have converted, all Israel will be saved. God's determination to save, therefore, cannot be defeated even by the refusal of some. On the contrary, Israel's refusal occasions the outpouring of God's mercy to the entire world. We could call it cosmic mercy.

Until now, we have considered Paul's evaluation of his experience and his vision in his own words. Now, in the Acts of the Apostles, we see the event through the eyes of Saint Luke. He relates Paul's encounter with the risen Christ three times!

Artists have reveled in Paul's being knocked off his horse. There is no horse mentioned in the text, only that Paul was thrown to the ground by a blinding light. But if indeed he was commissioned by the high priest, it is likely that this conveyance would be appropriate to his status. Falling off a horse is not pleasant and can cause serious injury. I fell from a horse twice before I was a teenager. The first time, I was riding bareback on Tommy, a heavy bay horse. When he stumbled, I fell forward, landing in front of his churning feet. How he managed to swing his heavy feet to avoid me I will never know, but Tommy chose to protect me. Even my horse, Tommy, practiced mercy!

The second time the horse had no intention of protecting me at all. Across the river I had a girlfriend everybody knew as "Doodlebug." She had a petite horse, whose name I've forgotten. One day when I arrived, she was mounted and invited me to mount behind her. That was fine with Doodlebug but not with the horse. He kicked up his hind legs, twisted, and sent me landing on my left shoulder and eating dirt. The only injury I felt was my wounded male pride. (Doodlebug and I chose different paths. A devout Catholic, she reared eight children, and after seventy years, I was able to reach her by phone on her deathbed.)

Neither of these experiences corresponds exactly to what Paul felt. He was blinded by an overpowering light that threw him to the ground. He could not see the speaker, but he could *hear* his voice: "I am Jesus, whom you are persecuting" (Acts 9:5). Not only has Paul met the Messiah in glory, but he also knows that Jesus's followers are one with him. They are the mystical Body of Christ, as Paul will later detail.

Luke's description of Paul's encounter with Christ agrees with Paul's understanding of it as a revelation of Christ in glory. Jesus's words "It hurts you to kick against the goads" (Acts 26:14), evoke the pointed instrument used to prod the draft animal to move. Sometimes a defiant animal will kick against the goad fruitlessly, hurting itself in the process. I am reminded of the Iowa farmer in a wagon, driving a repeatedly balking mule. When the mule had exhausted the farmer's patience, the farmer grabbed a pitchfork in anger and held it an inch away from the mule's tail. The next balk was the last one that mule ever did. The image that Jesus uses has the following meaning: "Paul, your resistance to Christ is only fruitless and harmful to yourself."

If we were able to trace the origins of our spiritual genealogy, many of us would thank Paul for making God's mercy available to us.

Mary Magdalen

In Saint Mary Magdalen's parish, where I resided, it was customary on the saint's feast day, July 22, to place her statue on the altar rail, conspicuous enough to focus attention appropriate to her feast. As the other priests and I were vesting for the morning Mass, we heard a commotion in the church. A young man had approached the statue, paused a moment, and then attacked it, sending the plaster saint crashing across the sanctuary floor. Mary Magdalen was beheaded and dismembered. A swarthy parishioner rushed forward, tackled the culprit, and sat on him until the police arrived. The young man was not trying to add martyrdom to the saint's credentials, though the remains on the floor looked like it. His problem was mental illness combined with recent attendance at a fundamentalist church that condemned statues as idols.

It was another of the fates to which this woman disciple of Jesus has been heir since her appearance in the Gospels. The certain things the evangelists tell us are that Jesus had cast seven devils out of her, that she was one of the women who followed Jesus, that she was with the mother of Jesus and the other women at the foot of the cross, and that she was the first to see the risen Lord and tell the good news to the disciples. The less certain things we know of her, though, have been added to her memory. The woman of bad repute who washed Jesus's feet with her tears and dried them with her hair is not named, but Christian tradition has assumed it was the Magdalen. Sometimes the unnamed woman caught in adultery is presumed to be Mary Magdalen. France claims to have her tomb; other places claim her veil; and of course, novelists have reveled in the thought that she was married to Jesus, which says more about the prurient imagination of the authors than it does about history.

Statues of Mary Magdalen, like ours—now restored in the church—present her with long flowing auburn hair, recalling her presumed former profession as a prostitute, holding a cross, with a vial at her feet to recall her anointing Jesus and a skull to suggest the tradition that she spent the rest of her life in solitude and penance. Of course, the cross truly recalls her presence at Calvary. But less valid are the other items. I will not dispute the assumptions of Christian piety, but if I were going to commission a statue of Mary Magdalen, I would show her running as if flying, her eyes wide with excitement unmatched by the runner from a marathon crying, "Victory!" For hers was a cry of victory, and more: He's alive! It was this role as the first herald of the good news that the early church remembered most about this woman. And I doubt very much that this herald would spend the rest of her life in retirement. How could she not keep shouting the good news wherever she went?

Why would the apostles, in proclaiming the resurrection of Jesus, make such a fuss about her role? Because it was so countercultural, and so much the kind of thing Jesus would do. Countercultural because in the patriarchal order of those days, the testimony of women was always subject to doubt. Even the disciples found it difficult to believe her and had to find out for themselves. Perhaps they even felt slightly miffed that Jesus had passed over them, the male leaders. But honesty prevailed in the gospel accounts. It was a woman, and it was Mary Magdalen!

To appear first to a woman—and to Mary Magdalen of all women—is also precisely the kind of thing Jesus would do. And here we run into the problem of another invention of Christian piety, the belief that Jesus would have appeared first to his mother—she, who was the lone human responsible for the body nailed to the cross; who nursed him as a child, lived thirty years with him; who suffered compassion at the cross as no one else could have; and who held his limp body taken from the cross. How could Jesus *not* have given her the consolation first of seeing him risen?

I asked myself those questions, until one day a different question came to my mind. If Jesus had asked his mother her preference, what would she have said? Mary more than any understood the mission of Jesus. He came to call sinners, he came to lift the lowly, and to proclaim the good news to the poor. She had said so much in her song to Elizabeth: he has lifted up the lowly! How could she not want Jesus to appear first to the lowest, the sinner, the one who had been most in the devil's trap, the one who needed the good news most, the last who would become the first. "Yeshua, Mary Magdalen should be the first to see you risen!"

In our Christian tradition, Mary Magdalen is the icon of mercy received. That's because we often picture her as a former prostitute who received God's mercy the moment she first met Jesus. Whether prostitution was one of the seven devils Jesus cast out, the fact is that meeting Jesus was meeting mercy. She was changed; she became a disciple and a model for all repentant sinners. But Jesus had an even greater role in mind for her. The crowning gift of Jesus's mercy was when he chose her to be the first to see him risen. His mercy would make her more than a disciple. It would make her first witness and evangelist. On the one hand, it shows that the converted sinner is not a second-class citizen in the church of Jesus. If that were the case, we would all be second-class citizens. On the other hand, it shows that those the world might consider least worthy can become the most worthy, for it depends on God's gift, and nowhere does God's mercy shine so brightly as when the sinner is transformed not just to be a disciple, but to be an evangelist. Peter had every reason to expect rejection by Jesus, but the Lord chose him to head the church.

Jesus's choices seem crazy by human standards. But there is a lesson here for all of us. If Jesus were invited to a reception today for a VIP, where and with whom would he spend most of his time? Would he want to be photographed with the VIP? I rather think you would find him visiting with the wall flowers, maybe even with the servants, the "second-class citizens." Yes, he would evangelize the VIP, as he did with the Pharisee who invited him to dinner, but he would point out the beauty of the prostitute proclaiming her repentance, the one who in Jesus's eyes is the real VIP. Pope Francis has so strikingly said, "The center is best seen from the margins."

The Mother of Mercy

I have learned to live my life among sinners because I am one of them. But I wonder what it would be like to live with someone who never contracted original sin and never committed a personal sin. That was Joseph's vocation on earth, and it will be yours and mine in heaven. But what would it be like living with them on earth? Not only was Jesus sinless—being the Son of God—but so was his mother. How did Mary act? How did she react when she opened the new earthen jar of wheat only to find it infested with weevils? Or at the market when some village woman scorned her because she had gotten pregnant before marriage?

It is easy to see Mary adoring her child in the Christmas crib or ascending in the glory of her assumption. But ordinary daily life at Nazareth? Catholics, formed by holy cards and statues, need a reality check about that. Did Mary ever sweat? Did her muscles ever ache? How did she handle starting the work week after the Sabbath? Did it or did it not burden her the way Mondays sometimes burden us? The Queen of heaven may have ivory hands in heaven, but she had servant's hands on earth.

She had only just heard the message that she would be the mother of God and took off "with haste" (Luke 1:39) to help her relative Elizabeth. She said she was the servant of the Lord, and servants serve. And servants of the merciful God are servants of his mercy. That is why at the annunciation she heard the whole message: not only that she would be mother of the Lord, but that her relative Elizabeth was also with child. The angel said nothing about going to help her, but Mary heard the news as a call to serve. After Elizabeth's praise of her, Mary bursts into her own praise in a song that has since been sung daily by the church for two thousand years: the *Magnificat*. More glorious than the strum of an angel's harp, it poured from the heart of a late teen flushed with joy that God has looked upon the lowliness of his servant (see Luke 1:48) Twice she hails the mercy of the Lord, once his mercy in coming to save Israel as he promised (see

1:54–55), and again "for those who fear him from generation to generation" (1:50), for the whole world.

The visit to Elizabeth was an act of mercy to one of Mary's own family. But we see a broader concern at the wedding feast of Cana. Some think Mary may have overseen the event, but that is doubtful since her words to Jesus, "*They* have no wine," instead of "We have no wine," indicate the observation of a guest alert to the needs of others. First, we have Mary's keen alertness to the needs of others—the initial step in an act of mercy, alertness to the other's need. My own mother was like that when we had guests for a meal. As soon as a guest finished an item on their plate, Mama would invite them to have another portion. That saved the guest any embarrassment they might feel at appearing greedy in asking for more.

Frank Rodarte, a daily Mass member of Saint Mary Magdalen parish, saw and responded to a more serious need. Driving home from a concert in a cold, blustery night, he spotted a poor man covered only with a plastic garbage bag fighting the icy wind and rain. Other drivers might not have even noticed him. But Frank pulled over, got out of his car, and put his own heavy coat over the man's shoulders and walked him to a nearby coffee shop, where he made sure he had some inner warmth to match the coat Frank left with him. It's a deed that Jesus would have learned from his mother.

Whenever I recall this story, I repent of the times I was "too busy" or "in a hurry" to answer a brother's or sister's need. Why are we so often afraid to be inconvenienced?

At Cana, Mary did more than observe that the wine was exhausted and that the host would be embarrassed. She knew where she might get more in a hurry, and she also knew how to ask. A simple statement would be enough to alert Jesus to the need, and he had two gifts: mercy and power. She trusted that, if he knew the need, he would respond. He had not planned to open his public ministry that way, but Mary's merciful heart moved his and he did.

5

RECEIVING AND GIVING MERCY

The New Creation

Living on the ranch, our family experienced creation as a daily revelation. Sunsets turned clouds into glowing charcoals. Then, like a cosmic stage curtain, they soon opened to an evening symphony of stars. Night competed with day to present a revelation of beauty and goodness. Wildlife offered constant surprises. We were so confronted by a creation constantly disclosing its mysteries that logic more than faith told us that there was a God.

The awesome beauty of creation was accessible to us because the Creator had given us eyes to see the stars, ears to hear the brook, a nose to smell the rose, and even touch to caress it. Imagine what it would be like if we had no access to beauty! What would it be like if we could not see? If we could not hear?

That possibility came home to me when I was asked to speak at a catechetical conference in Dallas, Texas. It was in the sixties, at a time when guitars, now permitted for the liturgy, were drawing the Gregorian-choked young folks away from traditional organ-and-choir performances and ruffling the feathers of those who could not imagine such trashing of the sacred. So, if you are going to offer a Mass at a conference with such divided tastes, what do you do? You offer the choice of both styles of Masses at the same time. So, Joe Wise strummed his guitar to the "progressive" congregation at the Mass in one hall, while I preached to the "dignity-entrenched" congregation at the Mass in another.

As I joined the procession into the hall, a symphony of voices boomed out to the cadences of a classical organ. I could have been in a cathedral. Approaching the sanctuary, I spotted a person facing the congregation and apparently giving directions with his hands. I assumed he was encouraging the crowd to join in the singing. But no, on closer inspection, I realized that he was signing to the deaf. And then it struck me. These folks had never heard the beauty of sound. Never had they heard music. Never had they heard singing. Never had their baby ears heard their mother's lullaby or father's laughter. In place of the magnificent sounds of the choir that had so enraptured me, they could only see moving hands.

As the Mass progressed, I could not get my deaf brothers and sisters out of my head. I was sobered by the gift of hearing that I had but they did not. Again, the mystery of inequality haunted me. Here I was, having grown up in a home where music was as much our language as speaking. Perhaps by never hearing, they were spared the agony of losing something they once had. Regardless, I was humbled by the gift to which I realized I had no right: to be immersed in the world of music and song.

Did it ever strike you that each of our senses is a gift of God's mercy? Perhaps the mission of the deaf is to teach us to appreciate our gift of hearing. Perhaps the mission of the blind is to teach us what a gift it is to see. Perhaps the mission of anyone disabled is to call forth from each of us the compassionate mercy of Jesus.

Creation is like a beautifully painted Easter egg that the human mind can never crack. We cannot know the inner mystery of this God's life unless he himself breaks the shell and reveals the glory of his inner self. And maybe if he did, he would help us make sense of our humanity, which, for all its wonders, has its nights without stars and its days without sun. He did. The misery of self-scarred humanity won from this Creator God a new kind of creation that opened his heart as a door to infinite mercy.

The new creation began, as did the first, with light, but this time it was a voice speaking to a human heart. "Go forth," the voice said, and Abraham obeyed. It was the first page of a story that would climax with Jesus Christ, who cracked open the shell and showed us the inner mystery of God. He did it by showing us how to live a human life that finds its glory in the total donation of self, as was his own on a cross. On the stage of human history, he showed us the divine mystery of measureless love. It was a love that brought healing, but only enough to invite faith in the power of the risen Lord preparing us for bliss eternal. For the rest, he walked the path of suffering with us. He was the promise of our glory and the companion of our pain.

Thus, aside from the gift of creation that, in itself presents many questions, he revealed the face of God. The mysterious creator is *Abba*, dearest Father. And the creative breath of Father and Son is the Holy Spirit, the love of God poured into our hearts (see Rom 5:5). Once we have encountered that God, we can see all creation as a Father's love for his children. We see the stars as his kisses, the sun as his embrace.

Climbing in Nepal

If I had the time and a computer with endless space, I would tell the stories of mercy in the lives of the saints after New Testament times. I would tell of Augustine and of God's converting grace in the lives of others who had been great sinners as well as of those who are innocent from childhood, whose holiness was itself God's grace of mercy. But I will skip to my own experience of that mercy before passing on the stories of others today. Of the moments of mercy in my life, the outstanding ones are the close calls, two times when I could have died but did not.

Each year, we would take our novices on a ten-day trek into the foothills of the Himalayas, those giants the locals call the dwellings of the gods. Early October is the ideal time, for the valleys, lush with rice, host streams fed by waterfalls from the hills, and fresh snow blankets the jaw-dropping views of the highest mountains in the world.

We were halfway on our trek to Langtang. In the "hotel"—more a shelter on the way—that we had reached by Saturday afternoon, we decided to celebrate Mass before dinner so that we could get an early start on Sunday morning. The next morning, I was the first one up at 5:00 a.m.; I began stuffing my backpack with remnants of the night before. I held up a small plastic bottle of red liquid, and thought, *That's strange. I thought I consumed all the wine last night.* Then, thinking that it was still the unfinished wine, I consumed several swallows. It was a strange tasting wine. Then it struck me, *O my God! I just drank iodine! I just drank poison!* It was indeed Lugol's concentrated iodine that we had brought to purify a canteen of our drinking water.

Suddenly, I went through the stages of grief that Kübler-Ross outlines in her famous book, *On Death and Dying.* Stage 1. *Denial.* No, that really didn't happen. I really didn't drink poison. I'm not going to die. That illusion did not last long. Stage 2. *I did.* I drank iodine. Stupidity! Beating myself for doing this. What would our French Brothers say: "Stupid Americans, they don't know the difference between Bordeaux and iodine!" Stage 3. *Bargaining*. Here is where the famous doctor missed a step. I immediately thought of the words of the Gospel, "If they drink any deadly thing, it will not hurt them" (Mark 16:18). That called for prayer. By now everyone was up and confused by what had happened. I called them together. Holding hands, we asked Jesus to be faithful to his words. He was. I felt no burning in my stomach. I ate a normal breakfast, and the only tragedy was that we had no water purifier for the rest of the trip. Was it a miracle? I don't know, but it did lead me to confront my mortality, to thank God for the life I had enjoyed, and to think of meeting my Savior and Judge. Grace came in what appeared to be a close call. And if a miracle, it was a confirmation of Jesus's promise to take care of his foolish followers like me. His mercy spared me.

The other close call was on another trek in Nepal. Climbing and contouring in a rain that began at noon, we worked our way through a rainforest. An umbrella is quite adequate to handle trekking in the rain; otherwise, it doubles as a walking stick. At approximately two o'clock, I could hear the thundering of a large waterfall. I soon rounded a bend, and there it was, coming out of a heaven that I could not see and plunging into an abyss the bottom of which I could also not see. Awestruck, I paused to let my brothers pass, then took out my camera to photograph the last two novices crossing the narrow footbridge made of two split logs.

Replacing my camera, I worked my way to the logs, crossing on them gingerly and safely. But at the extremity of the logs was an obstacle I had not counted on—two slippery rocks. I put one foot on the first rock, noting the waterfall plunging below. Was it fatigue? The altitude? Or my trifocals? Before I realized, I was airborne headfirst and backward. Then two heavy blows to my left leg and arm, followed by a blow on the head. The thought of plunging hundreds of feet below was flashing through my mind, when suddenly I realized I was not moving. I was being held in someone's arms and another arm was reaching out for mine. I was conscious and, despite biting pain, I was able to reach the hands that were pulling and pushing me to safety.

What had happened? In a flash of angelic intuition, novice Basil had sensed imminent disaster as he watched me step on that first slippery stone. Quickly, he stepped out into the cascading water, found a rock to support his foot and was there in time to catch me.

"I wasn't sure the rock I found would hold both you and me," he said later. "I was afraid we might both be carried away." He was right. Basil is much lighter than me, and I was carrying a backpack, umbrella, and camera case.

What do you say when you realize you've had a brush with death and that you may well owe your life to a young man who risked his life to save you? Trying as much to break the pall of silence that had fallen over the group as to confirm the good news, I heard myself say, "Thank you, Basil, for saving my life," but the words sounded as inadequate and superficial as the water bouncing off those slick stones. I was still stunned with mystery. The Lord's promise by the Psalmist had just been fulfilled in my life:

> For he will command his angels concerning
> you
> to guard you in all your ways.
> On their hands they will bear you up,
> so that you will not dash your foot against
> a stone. (Ps 91:11–12)

My novices were his angels.

My life was spared but there were more risks ahead. As soon as I verified that I could walk and that the only bone fracture, if any, was my left elbow, I told the group we should move on. We did, spending the next half hour in silent prayer. Vimal had asked if I wanted to clean my wound, but I said I'd wait till we reached our day's destination. That was a mistake, as the next days would confirm. My left shin was bleeding and already swollen, and my left elbow was paining me sharply and dripping blood.

At 4:30 p.m., we came upon a village strung out along a razor-backed ridge. This was Syabru, our destination for the night, where we set about cleaning my wounds, while nature treated us to the most beautiful double rainbow I had ever seen. Only when I crawled into my sleeping bag did the shock of the afternoon hit me, as I shook and shivered for several minutes before falling to sleep.

The first to rise in the morning, I opened the wooden window and exclaimed, "The mountains are out!" which was even more effective than a rooster crowing to rouse a trekkers' dorm. The view was the peaks of Tibet. A few moments later, we stepped outside and looked eastward up the valley at the western peak of Langtang bearing down on us like some monstrous cock's comb.

I was in considerable pain, but after some hesitation decided to go ahead with the group. Del had purchased an umbrella to replace the one I had lost in my fall, but ten minutes on the trail I stepped on it and broke it. A walking stick substituted temporarily, and I could only hope it would not rain. The going proved tougher than anticipated, but when Vimal took my backpack and strapped it to his, I was greatly relieved. It was decided that Vimal and Doss, those with the most energy, would move on ahead and try to secure lodging for us at the shelter euphemistically called "Lama Hotel." It was tougher going from then on, and shortly after we crossed the bridge over the roaring Langtang Khola, it began to rain. What seemed like an interminable climb ended at 3:30 p.m. when Lama Hotel came in view and Lazarus, Edmon, and Santosh came out to meet us with umbrellas.

"Beds?" I asked, thinking of the many other drenched trekkers I had seen heading for this one refuge. "Did you get beds?"

"No," came the reply, "but we have a place to sleep."

The meaning of that enigmatic answer became clear a few seconds later as I found myself in a combined woodshed and chicken house, where the rest of our troop was already huddled around a fire. A space on the floor had been cleared and covered with a bamboo mat on which all nine of us would spend the night piled together in our sleeping bags like suckling shoats. The fire dried our clothes and a cup of hot tea along with the ludicrous situation of bedding down with chickens buoyed our spirits. The arrival of a lady vendor of Tibetan head bands provided entertainment as I bargained with her for a beautiful handwoven band I could use as a stole. I delighted in pointing to my multiple bandages and feigning histrionics to convince her that the high price was adding insult to my injuries. By the time we agreed on a "last price," everyone, including the lady, was chuckling. We made immediate use of the stole as we celebrated Eucharist there in the woodshed of Langtang Valley.

For me it was a Mass of thanksgiving. The Gospel reading of the grateful Samaritan leper was most appropriate for expressing our thanks to the Lord for being saved from disaster.

The night was a miserable one for me, not because of the cramped quarters and the chickens roosting on the woodpile next to us, but because of a new element that I had not counted on, one that would change the story of our trek. Fever indicated that an infection was settling in my arm. Next morning, I could hardly stand without support. The decision was imposed upon us by the facts: go back to civilization and get medical help as quickly as possible. If not, I might lose my arm, which I might anyway, even if I went back. There was no alternative, though, to a full day's walk back to Syabru, so next morning, helped by Basil, who generously decided he would forego the goal of the trek to be with me, I began working my way slowly back to Syabru. Exhausted, I told Basil we would not move at all the following day but would rest. Some German trekkers offered me some appropriate antibiotic, which I gratefully accepted.

As the day of rest wore on, the problem of the next move became more pressing. My arm was swelling badly, and I was in no condition to walk. There were a couple of options. Hire a porter to carry me back to Dhunche for a bus? Upon inquiry we found out that it would take three porters to do the job, taking turns for one hundred rupees each. It was an exorbitant price but nothing like the one thousand rupees the group demanded after a village scoundrel got into the picture and cowed the others into exploiting our desperate situation. Rescue by helicopter? It is done in extreme cases, and though expensive, it would save us the three days it would take to get back to Kathmandu by porter and bus.

There was indeed a military post at Syabru provided with a shortwave radio. Basil was given a warm reception by the soldiers there, and a detachment of them even came down to the hotel to see me, offer their sympathy, and promise to send a message to Dhunche the next morning, whence it would be relayed to Kathmandu and on to the American Embassy.

That evening, Basil and I prepared a carefully worded message asking the embassy to contact Saint Xavier's School to get the prepayment that I was told was essential, identifying myself as a Catholic priest teaching in Kathmandu, and so on. Then, with the help of two English-speaking Nepalis, all of this was put into Nepali and next morning given to the radio operator. Basil and I waited. Finally, about 11:00 a.m., the head of the army detachment came into our room. With a face full of pain and embarrassment, he informed us that they had been unable all morning to make radio contact with Dhunche. The day passed without further success, and now the seriousness of our situation was beginning to dawn on us. At length, we decided that Basil should himself take the message to Dhunche the next morning. That meant leaving me unattended as he made the five-hour journey and would probably not make it back by nightfall. At this point we had no other option.

That night I had a heavy sweat. Getting up to put on the only dry clothes I had, I reflected that I could use the next morning to dry my clothes in the sun. But the day dawned cold and rainy. Feeling cold, I got up and worked my way to the kitchen where I expected a fire, but I was a half-hour early. After breakfast, Basil hastened to the military post to get their letter of explanation to take to the military in Dhunche. I expected him back in minutes. Time wore on and he did not appear. Meantime, the lady manager came in to sweep our room. Preferring to avoid the dust, I got up and stood outside until I saw her gathering her pile of dirt near the door. On top of it was my box of antibiotics that the Germans had given me. I quickly retrieved it, but that little incident was like the last straw. I went back to my bed and did the most serious praying of the entire journey, like the cry of Job and Saint Teresa's, "Lord, if this is the way you treat your friends, no wonder you have so few!" I should have still been in the glow of wonder at my rescue from the waterfall, but how easy it is for a burst of religious experience to be clouded by a series of reversals, leading to the Psalmist's cry of desperation, "You have lifted me up and thrown me aside!" (Ps 102:10). Still, somewhere amid my cry, I was able to surrender myself and my immediate future to the Lord.

Basil, after a long time, burst into the room. "Good news. The operator got through just now to Dhunche. I won't have to go!" "Praise the Lord," I said, but I then realized that too much optimism would be ill-placed. Would the Dhunche radio work any better than the one in Syabru? And the message had been translated from English to Nepali. If Dhunche got through to Kathmandu, it would then be translated from Nepali back to English at the embassy. Would the embassy get anything more than the shreds of my message? There was nothing now to do but hope, wait, and pray. At best, we could expect a helicopter the next morning, six days after the accident.

After lunch, Basil and I were standing in the sun that was now breaking through. I was just getting ready to return to bed when we heard the whir of a helicopter.

"Your helicopter has come!" shouted the lady manager. My first reaction was disbelief. This can't be ours; it must be for someone else. By this time, however, the military chief came running: "Hurry up!" He also seemed relieved and indulging in some measure of pride at a successful accomplishment.

A well-dressed Nepali stepped out of the chopper and extended his hand. "I'm from the American Embassy," he said. "All we got was your name, terribly misspelled, your passport number, and the place, Syabru. But we got the military helicopter to come at once."

As we lifted off, I felt it was all still a dream. The only thing I remember of the flight was the confirmation it gave me of these precipitous Himalayan mountains. I thought we were flying over church spires. Twenty-five minutes later, we were met at the airport by an embassy official and whisked in an embassy car to a clinic that was awaiting our arrival. Within an hour, the best osteopathic surgeon in Nepal had operated on my left elbow to drain the abscess. By 5:00 p.m., having been given heavy medication for my recovery, Basil and I walked into our home in Kathmandu.

I had cried to the Lord "out of the depths," and he had heard my prayer. He had mercy on me, but the hands he used were the hands of my novices. Basil had saved my life and stayed with me faithfully during the entire ordeal. At one point I asked him, "At the foot washing during our last retreat, whose feet did you wash?"

He paused reflectively, "Yours."

"That was prophetic, wasn't it? The Lord took you seriously."

But there were other hands the Lord used—the German trekkers, the gracious and helpful Nepali army, the helicopter pilot, the doctors at the clinic, and the American Embassy that did not wait for a prepayment but moved swiftly to the rescue. How glad I was to be an American! These were angels in the flesh, yes, including the playful angel who threatened to trash my antibiotics.

But the question, "Why me?" keeps returning. The mountains of Nepal, particularly Everest, have claimed hundreds of people who did not have rescuing angels. In 2015, at 11:15 on a Saturday morning, an earthquake claimed the lives of over eight thousand amazing people of that beautiful land. And what of the thousands of soldiers killed in wars? People tell me that I'm lucky to be alive. No, not lucky. Chosen. Chosen to remain, like the beloved disciple who lived on while Peter was crucified in Rome. After Jesus's resurrection, Peter asked Jesus concerning the beloved disciple, "Lord, what about him?" Jesus said to him, "If it is my will that he remain until I come, what is that to you? Follow me!" (John 21:21–22). Peter did just that—to the cross of Nero, while John remained, tradition tells us, the only apostle who was not martyred and died of old age.

It is not ours to crack the mystery of life, the why of its gift or the why of its length. If we cannot get our minds around the mystery, it is better to surrender before it and, like Job, confess that we do not know. But we do know Jesus and the Father, and before the mystery that is in their hands, we fall in adoration and confess their mercy. Whether we are Peter or John, we hear Jesus telling us every day, "Follow me."

6

REFRESHING MERCY

My older brother, Bruce, told me the unusual story of his first (and second) confession. Coached by a Sister of the Incarnate Word in the little country school in our hometown—she had even suggested some sins he might not have thought of—he nervously recited what his seven-year-old conscience and the Sister told him to say. After receiving absolution, he left the confessional, knelt in the pew, and recited the prayer the priest had given him as a penance. As he filed out of the church with the other boys, he was unaware of a small tear in the back of his shirt till suddenly he felt a finger slice from the tear to the shirt's tail. He swung around, popped the offender with a blow of his hand and thus began a fight with the shirt-slicing seven-year-old. When Bruce's aunt Margaret, who was helping supervise the first confession operation, saw what happened, she exploded, "Bruce, you are a bad boy. Go back to confession again." So dutifully, he went back, beginning, "Bless me father, for I have sinned. My last confession was ten minutes ago."

There are many funny stories about children's confessions, like the boy who confessed that he committed adultery, meaning that he had said a bad word he had heard only adults say. But such chuckle-ticklers are not common. I am convinced of the value of early confessions, for they are a great aid in forming the child's conscience. When I heard the first confession of one of my grandnieces, though I remember nothing of what she said, I was amazed at the sharpness of the insights of her conscience.

The sacrament of what we now call reconciliation is the water tap to which we may return for a new draft of God's mercy. I feel sorry for those Christians who do not have access to this refreshing spiritual bath. They often say, "I tell my sins to God, and I know he forgives me." I pray it may be so. But I wonder, both from a human point of view and from what I read in the New Testament. Psychologists tell us how good it is for us to share with another the things we are ashamed of. Long before modern psychologists, however, Jesus said to his apostles, "If you forgive the sins of any, they are forgiven them" (John 20:23). If the Pharisees were shocked that Jesus forgave sins, they would have been even more shocked when he handed on this power to men who themselves are sinners: "When the crowds saw it, they were filled with awe, and they glorified God, who had given such authority to human beings" (Matt 9:8; note the plural!). As a priest, I am often struck with trembling awe whenever I enter the confessional. The word *confessor* is most often understood as the priest to whom one confesses. But *confessor* means primarily the one who confesses the mercy of God on his own behalf, as Augustine did in his book *Confessions*. I enter the confessional as a sinner empowered in the name of God to pardon sinners. My head spins when I think of it. And when I leave the confessional, I never cease to be overwhelmed with the mercy of God for those I have confessed and for myself who is also a forgiven sinner.

I have heard every sin in the books, except for suicide successfully completed. The writers of *Cosmopolitan* and the tabloids who wallow in the shocking sins of celebrities would give a million dollars if they could sit in a confessional for just one hour.

Our job as priests, however, is not to explore the gory details of the sins confessed. All we need to know is just enough to classify the sin. I have no interest in indulging curiosity. I realize I am Jesus welcoming the sinner, and I am humbled by the penitent's humility in exposing their soul. That is what I too need when I ask another priest to hear my confession. Pride resists; yet surrendering to grace and baring the truth wins pardon and peace.

When a penitent says, "Bless me, Father, for I have sinned. It has been thirty years since my last confession"—no, that is not unusual—I don't register shock, nor give him or her the "tsk, tsk" treatment. Priests—at least those who have been around a while—

are incapable of being shocked. Instead, I give a welcoming smile and say, "Well, praise God, what a wonderful grace that you came today. Now what are the big things you want to ask Jesus to forgive you for?" Or something similar. Confession is a great homecoming, and what a privilege for us priests to be at the door with the Father's embrace. The word we use for the sacraments is *celebrate*. We *celebrate* the sacraments, and this applies with no less validity to the sacrament of reconciliation. It is the celebration for the prodigal who has come home; it is God the Father's homecoming party. So, who's afraid of a party, especially if you are the honored guest?

But there is something else special about this sacrament that makes it different from the others. Theologians tell us that each sacrament has two elements: matter and form. The matter is the material element— water, oil, bread, wine, and in marriage, the consent of the couple; the form is simply the words that are used—"I baptize you…This is my body…" and so on. Now in confession, the "matter" is our sins! If you don't have any sins to confess, it is not a sacrament. It's missing the matter. Amazingly, in this sacrament, God takes our sins and, through the words of absolution, turns them into the salve of our forgiveness and healing! Nowhere else is it so true that God makes all things work together unto good (see Rom 8:28). Yes, adds Saint Augustine, "all things, even our sins." Talk about mercy!

The Enemies of Mercy

There are two enemies of mercy: the self-righteous, who think they don't need it, and the self-condemning, who are convinced they don't deserve it. I'm talking about attitudes, not about actual needs. Everybody needs mercy, for all have sinned and been deprived of the glory of God (see Rom 3:23). But one's attitude toward mercy makes a significant difference to the outcome, either temporal or eternal.

The Gospels portray the Pharisee as the iconic self-righteous. In one account, the Pharisee boasts of his virtue to God's face, while the publican won't even lift his face (see Luke 18:13). The ego can feed on anything, even on one's religious observance, and that is what the Pharisee does. But we are often tempted to feed on less. It is easy to award oneself medals and trophies that others ought to bestow on us if they only appreciated our importance! For such a person, failing at something might be a real grace, a merciful provision of the God of truth.

That happened to me when I began teaching high school freshmen when I was twenty-one. Until then, I had either dodged things I might have failed in (e.g., when, as a high school freshman, I dropped football the first day of practice) or recovered from the sting of failing a geometry exam when all my other grades were in the middle or high nineties. But trying to control the stampede of boys in room 101 from September to May was more than this old cowboy could handle. Where's my horse? No, this was a stampede of a different kind. I considered the year itself a failure, although years later I met cultured gentlemen, into whom many of them had grown. I remembered plopping emotionally exhausted in a lounge chair at an end-of-year picnic, in which the seasoned teachers were chortling over beer and bridge.

But that year was filled with grace, as I see it now. It was humiliation that I needed. It was mercy. It prepared me for a powerful experience of mercy I was to have in a couple of months when a Marianist priest, Father Mike, asked the provincial to assign me to the school of which he was principal. He *asked* for a failed teacher to teach at his school! The day before class, he sat me down in his office and said, "Look, George, you have the makings of a good teacher. And there's no reason you can't begin tomorrow." Mercy sometimes comes when people tell you they believe in you in the absence of any guarantee. I became a surprisingly successful teacher that year, launched by the faith that Father Mike had in me. Despite Peter's failures, Jesus believed enough in him to say, "Feed my lambs...feed my sheep" (John 21:15–17). By his compassion and trust, Father Mike showed me the mercy that triumphs over judgment (see Jas 2:13).

The other enemy of mercy is self-condemnation. If the Pharisee is the icon of self-righteousness, the icon of self-condemnation is Judas. He announced his own guilty verdict to the priests: "I have sinned by betraying innocent blood" (Matt 27:4). But then without judge or jury and without a glance at the God of mercy and forgiveness, he decided to sentence himself and to carry out the sentence himself: he hanged himself. Was James perhaps remembering Judas wistfully as he wrote what Judas could not accept: "Mercy triumphs over judgment"?

None of us thinks of himself or herself as a Judas. But I know from my own experience and that of others I've met in the confessional, that there is in us not only a judge who announces our sin (thank God for conscience) but a court that applies the sentence and an executioner to carry it out. I'm not talking about doing penance for our sins. I'm talking about people who once forgiven, beat themselves up with guilt and try in some insane fashion to reverse their history: "If only I hadn't done that. That's awful. How could I have done that? O God, if only I could live that time of my life over." And so on. But life is not a tape that can be rewound and rerecorded. As Lady Macbeth said, "What's done is done."

The problem is that, as we grow older and get closer to God, the enormity of past sins also grows on us, and that increases the grief. Here is where Saint Paul comes to our aid: "For godly grief produces a repentance that leads to salvation and brings no regret, but worldly grief produces death" (2 Cor 7:10). Repentance frees; remorse binds. Rather than rollicking in the river of mercy, the soul prefers the desert of recrimination. This specifically applies to sins that are unknown to others, especially to those who would be shocked or pained to know, like one's spouse.

There is also the instance of a public revelation of what one hoped to remain hidden. A public figure falls like a lobby portrait trashed on a hotel floor. Seeing that it cannot be restored, some of those pictured there would incinerate it, that is, finish off the trashing by eliminating it. Many are those who, like Judas, cannot bear the shame and choose to destroy themselves instead. Hara-kiri, in one form or another, is not limited to the Japanese. The destruction may not be physical, but an inward self-mutilation that leads to depression, that worldly sorrow that Paul says leads to death. But our God is a God of exodus, a God of freedom, and a God of deliverance. He not only forgives when we repent, he wants us to leave the "Egypts" of our lives forever and to live in the promised land of mercy. God does not want any of his children to be a prisoner of their past. From the vase we have shattered, God will, if we let him, make a mosaic from the fragments.

After a night of repentance and spiritual renewal at a retreat I preached in Patna, India, several retreatants shared what they had experienced the following morning. One gentleman said that he had a dream in which a deer was standing within a rope that had once bound it but had now fallen to the ground. The deer continued to stand there, either unaware of its freedom or fearful to step out of the rope—a beautiful image of the forgiven sinner who remains trapped in the bondage from which he or she has been freed.

Leave the rope, leave the bondage! "For freedom Christ has set us free. Stand firm, therefore, and do not submit again to a yoke of slavery" (Gal 5:1). In this case, it's not that the soul wants to return to the sinful life; ironically, it must choose whether remorse will keep it there.

7

IN THE NAME
OF MERCY

My eighty-sixth birthday, which was only on the horizon as I began the first chapter of this book, arrived. In chapel, I began reviewing the blessings of my life, from earliest memory of my great-grandfather towering over me to the presence of the bread-looking God before me now in the tabernacle. Thanksgiving flooded me. God has gilded my life with graces and blessings so great that I feel like a chalice of gold. Even the rough times, the crosses, have turned to gold because each one of them taught me that God makes all things work together unto good for those who love him (see Rom 8:28). My thanksgiving was a reflection of the gold.

But then I said to myself, "But that can't be all. There are blotches amid the gold, my sins." "No," the Lord seemed to say, "Wherever there are blotches, they are the brightest bursts of gold."

"That can't be," I countered. "That's the one thing that has messed up the beauty of the chalice, and I did it, not you."

"So, you're still thinking of your sins? Why are they so important to you? You repented long ago, and you continue to repent when you fail. Where there was a blotch, I have covered it with my purest gold, my mercy."

"I'm still trying to rewrite my past to make it perfect."

"Yes, then you wouldn't have to tell me you're sorry, and I would have to love you because you are perfect."

"So, it's pride?"

"The worst kind. Spiritual pride. And most of all, it ignores my greatest gift, something I most delight in giving, my mercy. You would rather not need my mercy?"

"I must confess that I would rather not need it."

"So, who do you think you are?"

"I always wanted to be first in my class—better than the rest. I guess I applied my competition for grades to competition for holiness. I don't want to be classified as a sinner. But the fact is I am a sinner that is embarrassed by my sin. I wish I could erase it from the book."

"But I have erased it. More than that, in its place, I have written, '*Forgiven.*' My pen was the cross and the ink was the blood of my Son. Or, to put it in the language of the chalice, I have covered it with gold. You see, I love to create. And I love to re-create. You are my new creation. The problem is that you are not allowing yourself to experience the joy of being forgiven. Quit looking at yourself and see instead the infinite love I have for you. Your sin reveals my glory because it reveals my mercy."

"Lord, forgive my pride."

"Have you heard about forgiving and forgetting? Forgiving is a challenge at any age. But forgetting comes naturally when you get older, not so? Well, I've been around a long time. I'm older than any of my creatures. I'm busy forgiving all the time, and it's the privilege of my age to forget." I sensed him winking at me.

What he was really saying, I think, was that his loving embrace of me—the embrace of union—was more important than any slip along the way, and those slips recede into oblivion when I'm held in his arms. Mystic, saint, and doctor of the church, Catherine of Siena, who dictated her *Dialogue* in ecstasy, wrote, "'How great is the eternal mercy with which you cover the sins of your creatures!' I do not wonder that you say of those who abandon mortal sin and return to you. I do not remember that you have ever offended me."[1]

There is a story of a cardinal who, learning that a young girl was claiming she was receiving messages from Jesus, called her in to question her.

1. Catherine of Siena, *Catherine of Siena, The Dialogue*, trans. Susan Noffke, OP (Mahwah, NJ: Paulist Press, 1980). See Archdiocese of Detroit, "Saint Catherine of Siena on Divine Mercy—Homily," Unleash the Gospel, April 12, 2021, https://www.unleashthegospel.org.

"Does Jesus really talk with you?"

"O yes, Your Eminence." She had been coached to address him that way. "He talks to me every day."

"Hmm," mused the cardinal, pausing to think of a test he might give her. Finally, he said, "I want you to come back in a week. Ask Jesus what I said in my last confession and let me know."

The little girl cheerfully agreed. When she came back as agreed, the cardinal thought he had given her the perfect test.

"Well," the cardinal said. "Did you ask Jesus what I said in my last confession?"

"O yes, Your Eminence. I asked him right away."

The cardinal leaned forward with interest. "And what did Jesus say? What did I say in my last confession?"

"Jesus said he forgot."

There is more truth than humor in the story. Of course, God knows everything. The question is, does he care? That is the point of the story. Sins repented and confessed are like the cumulus clouds toward evening on a hot July day in Texas. They disappear; they evaporate. And if perchance they hang around, they turn golden red, trumpeting the glory of the setting sun. The Qur'an puts it beautifully: "There is no escape from God but to him" (Surah At-Tawbah 9:118). Somehow, it seems that we would like to stand apart and give God something that is truly ours. In fact, the only gift we have is something he has first given us. Our very existence is his gift. The air we breathe, the food we eat, even when we create something, it is never creation out of nothing. For us, "creation" is only a limping metaphor that falls terribly short of what God does when he creates. Even our ability to make something out of something is the gift of God who can make something out of nothing and anything out of something—like wine out of water. There is one exception, though. The only thing we can truly claim as ours—something that God didn't give us—is our sins.

An embarrassment? You bet. But God wants even that because he can make something out of anything, and if we let him, he will make something beautiful from this raw, this awfully raw, material. So let him have your sins. You can't hide them, and you can't escape. Surrender. Let the Creator create. The only escape from God is to him. Once you realize that, you understand mercy.

Tarawa and Nagasaki

It was twelve years since a spray of Japanese bullets had wiped out my brother, Charlie, and his entire squad, the first to land on the beach of Tarawa in the South Pacific. I was having the usual breakfast of bread and a café au lait in the international Marianist seminary in Fribourg, Switzerland. Across from me sat Joseph Muraoka, one of the handful of Japanese seminarians who seemed to be closest to us Americans, a paradox considering his people and ours had fought on opposite sides of the war. Joseph was a mystery, for he would never speak unless spoken to, and he seemed to be sitting on dynamite that might explode at any moment. At least that's what it seemed like to me.

Thinking he could use some cheering up, I asked him if he had heard from his family lately. He just shook his head and that was the end of the conversation. A fellow seminarian whispered to me, "Joseph lost all his family by the atom bomb on Nagasaki."

Thud. You don't hear from a family that's dead—all of them.

Suddenly, I found myself as speechless as Joseph. His people had killed my brother, and my people had wiped out his family. And here we were face-to-face with each other as brothers preparing for the priesthood. Emotions jousted through me—shock and compassion for Joseph, anger at war, and awe at Providence that put us at the same table that morning.

In my teenage years, when passions were strong about winning the war, I published a small newspaper where I reprinted an article from *Liberty* magazine, with one line that went something like this: "God, give us the sense you gave geese, the guts to hate." The article was not talking about hating evil but about hating the enemy. I deeply regret that mouthing of the mood of many of adult Americans embittered by losses of their loved ones. But that was not the mood of the heart of Jesus, even for those he drove out of the temple. "Love your enemies, do good to those who hate you." God, like the migrating swallow, knows no borders, nor does the church. God's children are everywhere, and the church, with a mother's heart, flies to the hurting, heedless of man's frontiers. Often those children get caught in the decisions of their leaders, in the games of their warlords as in the case of Japan. Some fall for the myth that launches aggression; others are coerced to comply. When sanity returns, mercy begins to heal and point to a better future. Joseph and I were part of that better future.

But prejudice against a people often lingers. Forty years after the war, one of my relatives would still never buy anything made in Japan, not so much because in his words it was "Jap crap," but because of what our family had suffered. His stance was symptomatic of the prejudice that often lingers in our hearts, often without our knowledge. Perhaps it is a survival mechanism from tribal days or even further back to the animal kingdom. I've seen it in horses. When an unfamiliar horse is let loose in a pen, the locals often become rattled and aggressive. It takes a while for them to settle down and accept the stranger. Yes, even horses have a comfort zone that can be threatened by the unfamiliar, just as it is true of humans.

But it doesn't have to be that way. Jesus reached out to the rejected, the marginalized, those who either caused discomfort to the established ranks or were avoided by them altogether. He showed us that the stranger need not be the enemy to be feared but a brother we haven't met. Joseph was the brother I hadn't met. This was what Jesus meant by mercy. Mercy meant eating with Matthew, the despised tax collector, and his buddies. It meant going to Zacchaeus's house. It meant touching the leper. It meant being ritually contaminated in the name of mercy. It meant having among his followers a woman delivered of seven demons. It meant letting a woman of ill repute wash his feet in the presence of the shocked Pharisee who needed to learn the joy of being forgiven. Jesus was the revolutionary of mercy!

And that is what he wants us to be. Is it uncomfortable? For most of us, including me, yes. We prefer to stick with the friends in our comfort zone. The questions Jesus wants us to ask ourselves before retiring each night are these: To whom did I reach out today? Who was beyond my comfort zone? To whom did I show the kind of love that does not expect a response in kind?

Is that way of living possible? Come with me back to the day that Jesus, having attracted the thousands by his healings, took a mountain for his pulpit: "When Jesus saw the crowds, he went up the mountain; and after he sat down, his disciples came to him. Then he began to speak, and taught them" (Matt 5:1–2).

Jesus raises the bar higher than the old law—give up anger, lustful thoughts, divorce, and yes, love your enemies. To whom does he address these expectations? Who are "them" whom he began to teach? Directly, the disciples; indirectly, the crowds. To the crowds, his words are invitations; to the disciples, they are commands. Why the difference? The crowds have made no commitment to Jesus, the disciples have: "his disciples *came* to him." They left the anonymous, miracle-fed crowd and stepped forward to identify with Jesus, to commit their lives to him. They are expected to live the new life Jesus proclaims. The crowds may very well say that to love one's enemies is impossible. But if they see it being lived by those who commit their lives to Jesus, they may very well think twice. Maybe it's not impossible. I see others living it.

But how do they do it? Not by their own power, not because it is law—though Jesus may look like a new Moses proclaiming law from the mountain—but because Jesus is in their midst in a way that Moses was not. We must wait to the end of the Gospel to hear it fully explained: *"Teaching them to obey everything that I have commanded you. And remember, I am with you always, to the end of the age"* (Matt 28:20). Jesus had been among his disciples during his public ministry. But now, risen from the dead, he is with them with resurrection power and not for a mere three years—but forever! He meant those words for us. Jesus does not expect us to do it by ourselves. He promises to be with us who have committed ourselves to him. We can do it. We can live the impossible dream because he, the risen Lord, is with us.

Into the Arms of Mercy

It has been some time—more than a year—since I finished the preceding chapter, never to touch the keyboard for the book until now. Something had mysteriously cauterized the passion that birthed the chapters I had written. I was unaware at the time that a priest of our archdiocese, one I had known for forty years, had just been named in a lawsuit by a "John Doe," who claimed that thirty years earlier the priest had molested him. The accused priest had pleaded not guilty, but the die was cast. I saw no connection between my writing paralysis and this event until what happened two weeks ago. Father Virgil committed suicide. He put a pistol to his head, fired, and slumped in his chair, his finger still curled on the trigger. Like many of his fellow priests, I slumped into a pit of my own, a pit of sorrow and confusion. How could this man, a brilliant theologian, internationally acclaimed for his breakthroughs in Hispanic American theology, so loved by so many, put such a tragic signature to a fruitful life?

The enormity of his suicide left me with a storm of emotions more than I could name—anger, grief at the loss of a friend and brother priest, shame because of the scar it left on the image of the priesthood, and possible scandal to those who might claim because of his action that suicide was acceptable. The *Catechism of the Catholic Church* ranks taking one's own life as the gravest of sins, with eternal, irreversible consequences. One of my university students, the daughter of an

Evangelical pastor, insisted in class that suicide is a sin that can never be forgiven. The self-imposed judgment by an act so final allows no time for repentance. The case will never be reopened. Mercy, she insisted, is denied.

Yes, objectively, suicide slams shut the gates of heaven and opens the gates of hell. But that judgment of an individual is not ours to give. Although we may have heard that in the Middle Ages, the body of the suicide was placed in crossroads where wagons from all directions might run over it, we have become more aware today of subjective elements that can lessen the responsibility for violent acts. "Grave psychological disturbances," says the *Catechism*, "anguish, or grave fear of hardship, suffering or torture can diminish the responsibility of one committing suicide" (§2282).

Nothing so plunges us into a cloud of unknowing as the loss of a loved one under such circumstances. For that reason, the church prays for those who have taken their own lives. She is a mother who has lost her son, a mother who has lost a daughter. And, like the mother who in her grief shook the corpse of her son who had committed suicide, crying "Wake up, wake up!"—a real case I reported in a previous book—she prays that somehow that son or daughter will one day wake with the rest of the disciples of the Risen One. That's because the church, like Mary, is the Mother of Mercy.

If we don't know how God's justice and mercy settle their claims in a suicide, we have more of a consolation when one dies blessed with confession and the sacraments. That can happen even in the case of a life-long sinner, such as the man to whom I was privileged to minister on his deathbed. He had years of sins on his conscience but had never confessed, and now he was about to face his judge. His face wretched with anxiety, but as I pronounced forgiveness, peace returned. Maybe he would undergo purification before seeing the face of God, but he sought mercy of the God who forgives. It is a gift to die in the embrace of mother church.

There are those who begrudge a man like that for slipping past the guard of justice and into the arms of mercy. They are not unlike the workers of the first hour who protest giving to the eleventh-hour hands what the full-timers have sweated all day to earn. To those I would say, Are you envious of his riotous life? If so, you are desiring sin. And desiring sin is sin. And unhappiness. Why not be a table partner of the pardoned and welcome the late comer? Bread and wine are still there in abundance, whether you come early or late.

The death of Virgil so touched my depths that it reopened the spring and pushed me to write. But there was another matter that primed the spring about the same time. And it was a happier one. The young adult members of our parish prayer group had turned a Thursday night's meeting into an hour of adoration of Jesus in the Blessed Sacrament. I have always had a special devotion to the Lord in his sacramental presence, ever since that teenage afternoon in Saint Mary's Church when this mysterious Other reached out of the tabernacle and grabbed me. It was an experience that sealed my call to the road less traveled, religious life. But this evening adoration bestowed a new grace for my twilight years. Has it ever happened to you that a truth of faith that you have known in your head all along suddenly strikes you with an overwhelming reality, like a spotlight cast on a darkened stage? Strengthened by my recent exposure to the miracles of Lanciano and Buenos Aires, where human flesh with an AB blood type appeared in a eucharistic host, I was hit as by lightning: Jesus is really here! It's as if someone who is spiritually present in your heart by love is suddenly standing in front of you. I knew already that Jesus is present where two or more gather in his name (see Matt 18:20). But that is his spiritual presence. By the miracle of the Eucharist, he is physically present wherever the consecrated host is. Body and blood, soul and divinity. Yes, it is under the form of a sacramental sign, but not any less real. The divine genius made our gathering for adoration as real as the crowds around Jesus at the Sermon on the Mount two thousand years ago. And that happens anytime, anywhere that people gather around his eucharistic presence. He is not satisfied being with us merely spiritually. He wants to be there physically, just as he was to the crowds in Galilee—or to his disciples in the intimacy of the Last Supper. Of course, now it is his risen, glorified body that is there, but one that can still be touched, as the doubting Thomas realized.

Talk about mercy! God is so madly in love with us that he wants to embrace us, flesh to flesh! And whether our tongue touches the host, or we gaze at him in the monstrance, he is there! All of him. And that's worth writing about!

Mercy to the Unwanted

Patti Tuttle and her husband, Dave, have fostered more than two hundred and forty newborns in their home. They have two biological sons and two adopted daughters, one of whom bears the name Kallie Marie. That was not the name originally given her by the police who found her wrapped in a paper bag next to a dumpster on a foggy San Antonio morning on January 27, 1989. They called her "Misty Dawn." When Dave and Patti heard her story on the news, they asked if they could adopt her, and they did. She is now a beautiful, successful adult, whose marriage at age thirty I celebrated in June 2019. They wanted the unwanted. And the unwanted became a gift to those who wanted her.

Is it possible to adopt a deceased baby? Dave and Patti did just that when they learned that a newborn baby girl was found stuffed in a toilet in Espada Park, San Antonio. The city authorities gladly gave them permission to take the body. They named the child Gloria Marie, and with a Mass that I celebrated, they buried her tiny body in the Baby Land section of Holy Cross Cemetery in San Antonio.

What must have gone through the mind of the young woman who dumped her baby like refuse to be flushed down the drain? Had she been raped? Had she yielded to her boyfriend because she wanted the love she did not have at home? Did she successfully hide her pregnancy? All we know is that she did not want her baby. But there are millions of other women who have chosen to rid themselves of an unwanted, inconvenient child. Men, whom nature has shielded from physically carrying the effect of their choice, and who often don't care, bear a similar responsibility. Strangely, the men do not have to invest in the emotional effects of their act the way women do. Women continue to shape the life they bear. That is why it is much more traumatic for the woman who decides to terminate the life of the defenseless person she has been growing.

No matter how God's justice must be satisfied, there are countless Christians who have rushed to fill the evil vacuum that is caused by an abortion, like John and Terry Haring, who run two pregnancy centers where they not only offer free pregnancy testing but also counsel couples toward adoption. There are foster homes, like that of Patti and Dave Tuttle, waiting to care for the child until adoptive parents can be found. For women who want to keep their child but fear they cannot provide for them there is the Gabriel Project, which assures pregnant women of diapers, baby food, and other necessities to raise their child.

So much for the pre-abortion works of mercy. Isn't after abortion too late? No. Women and men involved in abortion need healing of this self-inflicted wound, whether they come repentant shortly after the abortion or only years later when the full impact of their deed hits them. Project Rachel offers retreats to those suffering from remorse, which is their own form of PTSD. A retreat enables the participants to come to terms with their past, by giving and receiving forgiveness—forgiving themselves—which completes the forgiveness of God.

Jesus raised the daughter of Jairus, restoring her to her father. He raised the son of the widow of Nain, restoring him to his mother. To those still living he brought health. To the repentant he brought forgiveness, peace, and joy. Jesus was a life-giver, a compassionate life-giver. And he continues to inspire his followers to be the same. Nowhere today is the role of life-giver more obvious than in those who work strenuously to promote the cause of the unborn, to defend and promote life. It is the supreme work of mercy: to save life.

8

MERCY AND FORGIVENESS

Anger and Forgiveness

In my book *Living in the Father's Embrace*, I tell the story of Eric, the thirteen-year-old innocent victim of a drive-by shooting. He lay unconscious in a hospital bed surrounded by his praying family, all of whom pronounced forgiveness for the shooter, except for his aunt who stubbornly clung to her anger. The moment when she finally surrendered her anger and forgave, Eric stirred, began to regain consciousness, and ultimately was restored to complete health. Unforgiveness shackles healing; forgiveness clears the way.

Mostly, it is our own misery to which our unforgiveness keeps us bound. It may not always be physical illness that is caused by our unforgiveness; it may just be the misery we cause ourselves by holding someone else captive in our heart.

Remember Jesus's story about the king who had a servant who had fallen into such a huge debt that he was unable repay his master? His master ordered him to be sold along with his whole family and possessions to pay the debt. The servant fell to his knees, begged for more time (in modern terms, "extend the note"), and promised that he would repay the debt. In a moment of mercy, almost foolish mercy, the king forgave him the entire debt. The forgiven servant then went out and found a fellow servant who owed him a pittance and began to choke him, saying, "Pay what you owe me!" The previous scene is repeated as the debtor asks his creditor to be patient till he could pay the debt. But the creditor servant refused and had him thrown into prison until he paid the debt. When the king heard of it, he was so angry that he handed the unforgiving servant over to the torturers till he paid his original debt.

After hearing me proclaim this parable, a woman approached me and said she had been converted by the Word of God. She told me that when her husband returned from Vietnam, he was a changed man, exhibiting fits of anger, even physical abuse. On one occasion, he struck her on the head causing her bobby pin to stab deeply into her scalp. She took the pin, inserted it in a crack in the wall by the refrigerator where she could see it every day and remember what he did to her. It stayed there for twenty-seven years. Twenty-seven years fanning the flame of anger! "But when I go home tonight, I'm going to throw that pin away and forgive my husband." Twenty-seven years of anger wafted away by the words of the Spirit, "Father, forgive them, they know not what they do."

It is tragic that this refusal to forgive even grips entire nations. At a conference on peace, an Israeli minister once declared, "We will never forgive, and we will never forget." Is it any wonder that peace is so long coming? The entrenchment of anger between some Protestants and Catholics in Northern Ireland echoes Lamech's vow to boundless vengeance and Cain's, "Am I my brother's keeper?" Fortunately, there are, as there have always been, those who know better, who work for reconciliation and peace, and who know that the swords of the past can become the plows of the future. But that takes conversion, for the road to peace is traveled on one's knees.

Sometimes it is more than knees that hurt. Judy McCarthy, a friend of mine, was walking with Timothy Dowling, the eighteen-year-old leader of a march for peace in Northern Ireland when a shot was fired, killing Tim and grazing Judy's arm. She cradled his dying body and heard his dying prayer. On the radio, the young man's father pleaded for calm and said that only forgiveness would heal Ireland. Father and son had the same heart.

At Timothy's memorial service, held on the Feast of the Holy Innocents, Judy offered these reflections that speak for more than one peacemaker who has paid the price for peace:

I cannot pretend to make sense of the brutal murder of this holy innocent. But then I am also unable to make sense of the murder of the Holy Innocents during the time of Herod, or the condemnation to death of the Holy Innocent by Pontius Pilate. For murder—all murders—are senseless acts!

But what I can make sense out of is the life of this Holy Innocent. In the short span of eighteen years, Timothy Michael Dowling demonstrated more wisdom, courage, understanding and compassion than most men four times his age. For you see, Tim was a peacemaker.

Tim had a great devotion to Our Lady, and because of this, he possessed a unique characteristic that is common only to men who have a great devotion to Our Lady. Tim possessed that special quality that I like to call "the mark of Mary"—that special quality of gentleness Christ possessed, that special quality I suspect Jesus got from his mother, Mary—just as it was his mother, Mary, who taught him to pray. Tim was also a gentle man, that I expect he got from his mother, Katherine—just as his mother, Katherine, taught him to pray. You taught him well, Mrs. Dowling, because the last words he uttered were those of a prayer.

There is nothing more beautiful—and more powerful—than a gentle man. Paradoxically, gentleness encompasses the qualities of powerfulness and courage. Christ's power did not come from physical strength; his power did not come from domination over others, nor from repression and terror. Indeed, Christ's power came from his gentleness, his ability to be compassionate, his gift of giving them dignity as human beings. His was the strength and the power of courage, because to give others their dignity is one of the most courageous things anyone can do. That means standing up for the oppressed; defending the poor and the wretched; accepting their uniqueness, no matter what their religion or beliefs, no matter their nationality or country of origin, no matter their race or color. That means accepting each other not as my brother's keeper but as my brother's brother. Tim, like Christ, was a gentle, powerful, compassionate, and courageous man who was not afraid to stand up for the oppressed and the persecuted. Tim lived the belief that each was his brother and sister.

On the evening that Tim was killed, you asked me, Mrs. Dowling, if, amid all the violence, pain, and bloodshed, I could still see the face of Christ in others. The answer is an unequivocal "yes." Indeed, I had the privilege and honor of holding his broken and bleeding body in my arms. Christ was killed because he was a peacemaker. Like Christ, Tim was also killed because he was a peacemaker.

Saint Paul was right when he said that if we fail in love, we fail in all things. Tim did not fail in love, for there is no greater love than to lay down your life for others. And if it is true that love measures our stature, then Tim was a giant among men. Tim was a peacemaker.

Like all terrorists, those who killed Tim are, by contrast, very small, weak men; they are cowards! They hide and cower behind the false power of weapons because they are not strong enough to seek peace and harmony. They act out of fear; they are frightened that their own beliefs and standards are not valid, and so they seek to validate them through anger, and the terror and repression of others. Like Pilate, Herod, and Judas, they are weak, frightened men who are to be pitied. But woe to them who attempt to destroy peace, for peace is Christ's work! Tim did Christ's work because Tim was a peacemaker.

And as an honor to Tim, we will not seek revenge against these petty cowards, for

God will provide his own revenge. To seek revenge defies everything Tim stood for; it also defiles his memory. Instead, we resolve to be a people of faith in times of doubt, a people of hope in times of despair, a people of peace—an instrument of Christ's peace. We resolve to pray for those who injure us, to treat each other as our brother or sister—to see Christ's face in others. For then, and only then, can peace come. Like Tim, we will become peacemakers!

Thus, we will honor our gentle, courageous, and compassionate martyr with this Irish blessing: Tim, may the angels come to meet you, may the martyrs come to greet you, and may the Queen of Peace, whom you loved so much on earth, introduce you to her Son, the Prince of Peace, with these words: "Jesus, I'd like you to meet Tim. For like you, he was a peacemaker."

On October 27, 2013, the eve of her sixty-eighth birthday, Judy left this earth to join Tim and her other peacemaker friends. Physical therapist and bank courier as she was, until her health began to decline, she continued to travel to Ireland working for peace.

In his visit to Ireland Pope John Paul II said, "The key to peace is justice, but it takes love to turn it."

Healing

Viola was poor but she knew how to cook. She opened a little food service out of her garage, and when she had saved three thousand dollars, she opened a restaurant called *Los Barrios*. The word means "neighborhoods," but for Viola, it was the family name. Shortly the venture became one of the favorite eateries in San Antonio. Years later, her son Louie was able to open a three-million-dollar restaurant, *La Hacienda de los Barrios*. Even at the age of seventy-six, however, his mother stayed with the old restaurant, supervising the kitchen to make sure the food and service were perfect. But it was at that age that tragedy struck. A next-door neighbor just turned eighteen and was looking for money to feed his drug addiction. He broke into her home at night with a bow and arrow, shot and killed her, stole her credit cards and her Mercedes, and set the house on fire to cover up his crime.

A pall fell over the whole city, and at a Friday morning press conference, District Attorney Susan Reed, saying she might seek the death penalty, added, "I want to string him up myself."

But those were not the emotions of Louie. *San Antonio Express News* columnist Ken Rodriguez found him that evening in pain for Joe Estrada, the eighteen-year-old neighbor who committed the crime. "I can't stop praying for the guy," he said, "I'm real concerned for him. Can you imagine what he's going through? This child just turned 18. He's in for the most horrifying life you could imagine. My mother suffered for a few minutes. There is no way she would want what's going to happen to this man in a penitentiary. She will spend an eternity in heaven, but he will face a hell on earth."

The columnist was speechless. He said that he had never thought of the other side of the story. The Barrios family offered to pay the court costs for Estrada's defense, but the law would not allow it. As Viola's body was laid to rest, Louie and his sister Diana embraced Joe and Dorothy Estrada, the parents of the murderer. The rest of San Antonio saw it on the front page of the next morning's paper. If the murder stunned the city, even more so did their forgiveness.

Perhaps it was the speed with which the forgiveness came. That hardly seems normal. Maybe after months or years you might be able to forgive the one who murdered your mother. But this was a special grace, and it spoke loudly to the world. Violence, even the violence of hate, is no answer to violence. If forgiveness happened quickly, it was not quicker than that of Jesus during his pain from the cross: "Father, forgive them; for they do not know what they are doing" (Luke 23:34). What Jesus and Louie focused on was not what had been done but what had been left undone and what still needed to be done. Grief was crushing Louie, particularly because he and his mother were very close. But grief would not bring his mother back to life, and it would work itself out with time. In Louie's mind, as with Jesus, there was a more immediate need, a more pressing agenda. Jesus had taught forgiveness; now was the moment to live what he taught. It was also important to build a dam against the flood of hatred building in his disciples toward those who killed their Master. No, Jesus was saying, don't let this crime turn your hearts to hate and revenge. Let love heal your heart first so that you can be a healer for others.

Healing. That was the immediate agenda for Jesus and for Louie. Some would say you need time to feel the depths of the wound before forgiveness is real. Maybe so. But suppose your reserve of love is so great that it does not need time. Suppose grace did not wait on time and even saw delay as a useless distraction, an enemy of divine love? Suppose Louie had learned from his mother of a compassion that would flow to the one who is in greater need? Although we have no record of Viola's last words, her life spoke the kind of last words that another woman, Diane Tilly, a schoolteacher in San Antonio, breathed to the teenager who had robbed and shot her, "Bless this child."

The African American church in Charleston that welcomed Dylann Roof as a white, fellow pray-er for an hour, then lost nine members to his shooting, stunned the nation with a message of forgiveness. Nadine Collier, whose mother was one of the slain, said to the shooter, "You hurt me. You hurt a lot of people. But God forgives you, and I forgive you." Bethane Middleton-Brown, the sister of one of the victims, said, "I acknowledge that I am angry. But she taught me that we are the family that love built. We have no room for hating."

Jesus sometimes gives that grace, like his, out of the very pain it suffers. Love, great love, is like that.

Reflex Mercy

Rodney Buentello was no ordinary Marine. A master sergeant who had survived four combat tours—one in Afghanistan and three in Iraq—he twice received the Purple Heart. Now forty-two and retired, he reveled in treating his wife, Lisa Marie, and two sons aged eight and nine, to a favorite park flanked by the Medina River in Bandera, Texas, an hour's drive from their home in San Antonio. A modest dam gifts the river that feeds the dam with lake-like depths that also provide a swimmer's delight, as long as you stay far enough above the dam. For the dam is not only a creator of beauty and joy; it is a killer that has taken the lives of teenagers daring to challenge the plunging waters beneath the dam. Unknown at first, the waterfall creates a suction that traps the victim. After the first death, a sign quickly bellowed forbiddance: "Danger of Death!"

Whenever Rodney parked his van, it was always far enough up the river that his sons would not think of floating over the dam or even toward it—a safety measure reinforced by their father's prohibition.

But on June 8, 2016, something moved Rodney to park closer to the dam. There was no obvious reason for doing so, as his family could attest. And Rodney, himself, would probably not be able to explain it. But after piling out of the vehicle, they heard shouting and screaming coming from the dam. A young girl daring the odds had begun walking atop the dam. What was in her mind? Daring disobedience? Born of the tragic history of the spot, a sign with a skull and crossbones symbol glared: "STAY OFF DAM. No Swimming, No Fishing, No Walking on the Dam!" One often cannot fathom a teen's logic—or lack of it. At the beginning, the water coursing over the dam near the shore was gentle enough to tell her she could make it across. But the force toward the middle carried her in a second over the dam into a churning vortex. A lad seeing the girl's plight dove into the water and grabbed her, pushing her free, only to be trapped by the suction himself.

Rodney's mind instantly photographed the crisis. Without hesitation, he rushed to the dam, dived in and swam with violent speed to the victim. Amazingly, he was able to free the lad from the vortex.

But Rodney, who had survived bullets and bombs in Afghanistan, was felled by water. Having saved the lad, the decorated Marine drowned.

Stories of rescuers becoming victims have often been recorded. What gives me pause here is the immediacy of Rodney's response. No hesitation. No calculation. No questioning why someone else should respond. It was an instant response. I call it a reflex rescue, a reflex mercy. Some psychologists may claim that such a reaction is compulsive and hardly a human act. That is not fair to Rodney. There was a store of readiness in his heart. It speaks powerfully of the kind of heart that initially called him to join the Marines—to give of himself to serve. It kept him serving after the first Purple Heart and on to earn a second one. It reminds me of my brother, Charlie, himself a Marine. The attack on Pearl Harbor brought about his decision to join the Marines. Rodney was needed; Charlie was needed. Neither glanced around to see if someone else would go.

For both, there was a commitment to the absolute. They joined the toughest unit, determined to give their all—whether on a South Pacific beach where Charlie fell or, ironically, beneath a hill country dam where a survivor of battle wounds gave his life to save a lad.

Mercy has many forms. But it spurns measure.

9

PERSONAL STORIES OF FORGIVENESS

Making Peace—Robin's Story

It isn't easy when your dad leaves your mother to marry another woman. Your heart must learn to reset. This was the case with Robin, one of my students.

It was Valentine's Day, and my dad, who had married another woman, now had two hearts to love: his new wife's and my own. Since the marriage, things never went well between us two competitors for my father's love. Push came to shove on Valentine's Day. At school, I received a text from my dad telling me to find my Valentine's gift waiting for me at his house, and that he was taking his new wife out to dinner. Without a key to the house (I was living with my mother), I had to wait two hours, until my impatience finally seized me, and I called to find out why the delay.

He told me that his new wife had wanted more time with him. I exploded. "You should never have gotten married. I hate you!" I screamed and hung up. Days passed and I was so consumed with anger that I never spoke to him, even when he asked me how I was.

Five days later, as I was leaving school the text message came: "Your father passed away suddenly of a heart attack."

Five days later! Stunned by his death, I was more grieved because I would never get to take back my words of hate. Till this day—ten years later—I wish I could turn back time and pick up the phone and tell him how sorry I am. "Dad, please forgive me. I was an angry child." And what I would give to hear him say, "Robin, I love you and I forgive you!"

The whole event and its aftermath have made me think of Jesus's words, "Come to terms quickly with your accuser while you are on your way to court with him" (Matt 5:25–26). The problem is he got to court, God's court, before I did, not leaving me time to be reconciled, to embrace one another with a restoring hug.

I think of the five nights I went to bed angry, and I remember those words, "Do not let the sun go down on your anger" (Eph 5:26). Now the problem is no longer a problem with my father. It's my anger at myself, not just for the words I said but for not realizing how little time I had. Every night I cooked my anger, basting it with the memories of other hurts, even the smallest ones. But dad's life-clock was ticking and, before I knew it, both hands froze. Dad died, and with him, my chance of reconciliation.

I have tasted the poison of fist-held anger and I've found time to be treacherous, ready to vanish at any moment. I resolve to make peace with whomever I can before I go to bed. One never knows whether the eyes that you have closed tonight in earthly sleep will open to see the Golden Gate embossed with the words: "Only love enters here."

Keeping Faith— Angela's Story

My student, Angela, is the author of this story of losing a friend and nearly losing her faith.

On February 17, 2005, Michael Andrade was murdered in his apartment. Michael was a student at St. Mary's University majoring in biology. He was a son, a brother, a boyfriend, a colleague, and most of all, he was my friend.

I met Michael when he started working at Urban Ministries After School Kare. Our site was made up of all women, so we were all excited that we were finally getting a male co-worker. He was assigned to me to train him in everything I knew. After that first day, I felt like I had known Michael for years.

Like most friends, we had our inside jokes, we discussed the good and bad of our relationships, and we talked about other things that either bothered or excited us. Our friendship couldn't be anything but perfect.

One day, we parked by each other at school and walked to class together. We were joking around and laughing, and when we separated, his last words to me were, "See you at work on Friday."

Friday was early release, and when I got to work Michael was not there. I remember that the employees were upset because we were so short-handed. Nevertheless, we survived but all wondered where Michael was and wondered why he had not called.

When I got home, I decided to check my email. There was a bereavement notice, which I usually do not read, but something told me to read this one. As I was reading, I kept thinking, *Wow, all these things describe Michael*, but I pushed that thought aside not wanting to believe it. It finally hit me that it was Michael. The email did not say how Michael had died, so I asked mom if she had any news. My mom told me that she had heard something, but she did not know all the details. Later that weekend I found out that some guy broke into his apartment, there was a struggle, and that the intruder strangled Michael. He later set fire to the mattress to try to cover up the crime.

I was in shock and questioned God, wondering why God would allow this to happen. Why would he create people who hurt others? I was ready to give up my faith because I felt that God had let me down. I did not want to go to church or pray, for it no longer made sense. If God was such a loving God, how could this happen? People would tell me that Michael's now in a better place. How would they know?

Apostasy happens when people abandon their faith. I honestly came close to this. Before the tragedy, I never understood why people abandoned their faith, and I feel for those who do. In the end I did not give up my faith. Without my faith, I would still be hurting. I would still question everything, and I would not have anything. I still hurt when I think of what happened, but I know that I can go to church, light a candle, or just sit somewhere and think or pray. I know that Michael is watching over me and that he would not want anyone to abandon their faith. I would rather have my faith in my life than anything else.

All Things Work for Good—Hector's Story

Hector tells us how his faith has not only been strengthened by "three jarring experiences" in his life but how it has provided a framework for living it.

In my young life I have had three jarring experiences. The first occurred when I was only five years old. At that age, I had no worries. Life seemed perfect and joyful. What does a five-year-old have to worry about? But that's how old I was when my father left and divorced my mother. I was devastated. As a five-year-old, I could not understand how my father could leave mom and me alone. A woman of tremendous faith, my mother promised me everything would work out for the best. We moved in with my grandparents, where I spent some great years. I became closer to God thanks to my mother and my wonderful grandmother. It was a taste of heaven for ten years.

But the second jarring experience came when I was fifteen. My beloved grandmother was diagnosed with cancer. In those ten years with her, she had become an important part of my life, my second mother. She was strong in faith. Despite her knowing that she was going to die, she was never scared. Her faith helped me grow in my faith and become a better person. Whenever I complained, she would tell me, "Remember that someone in the world has it worse than you." And then she would quote Romans 8:28 in Spanish, the only language she knew: *Dios dispone todo para el bien de los que le aman.* (We know that all things work together for good for those who love God, who are called according to his purpose.) Indeed, that was the seal of her life as she went to the God whom she knew would turn even her death to good.

Three months later was my third jarring experience. My mother was sentenced to life in prison. She was in the wrong place at the wrong time and was convicted of a crime that she did not commit. This was the hardest trial of my life. I felt I had nothing to live for. I became extremely depressed and did not know where to go with my life. I was young and felt alone. My mother would write me and remind me not to lose my faith. "Remember what *abuelita* taught us. Everything will work out for good if we love God. Pray, *mi hijo*, and don't give up." Still in prison, my mother, to this day, has not lost her faith. She has become closer to God and has not given up.

Life has its ups and downs that we must face. What we can't do is lose our faith, our love for God. My grandmother and mother have both helped me to realize this.

Immediate Forgiveness— Aurora's Story

These stories of forgiveness present some contrasts—one that took twenty-seven years to forgive and others that happened gradually. We see forgiveness in the lives of many. But can forgiveness be immediate? Let me share Aurora's story.

On the evening of November 6, 2003, I was in the middle of praise and worship in the prayer group at Casa San Juan Chapel. A member of the group whispered to me that someone was at the door with an urgent message. To my surprise, it was my sister and nephew.

"Come with us at once, Aurora," they said.

"Where are you taking me?" I asked as I got into their car.

"We are going to Wilford Hall Hospital. Your family is there waiting for you."

That is all they said. They would not tell me what happened. The dreadful silence of unknowing gripped me for the longest half hour of my life as I prayed in the Spirit. At the hospital, they spirited me to the emergency room, where the first persons I saw were my daughter and my other sisters. My younger sister gently offered her condolences, but I didn't understand why. The hospital chaplain walked over to me, put his arm on my shoulder and said there was a shooting in the park where my son, Joseph, was playing basketball with his friends from work. The shooter shot Joseph's wife as she was walking. Seeing her collapse, Joseph ran to her. The shooter then shot him three times in the chest. He died at the scene.

"Who did such a horrible thing to my son? He was such a good man!" I said, and then, "I don't understand, but I forgive them." I don't know where those words came from, but later, I knew that it was the Holy Spirit, because I could not have done it on my own.

If I had not forgiven the killer immediately, I would be filled with anger and rage in my heart and that would have made me sick. I would not have been able to care for my son's ten-month-old child, Jaden, and his mother as she recuperated in my home for a year. My grandson has lived with me off and on since then and I help with his support. God in his mercy worked a miracle.

My prayer today is that I can stay in good health so that I can see Jaden graduate from high school and college.

If you felt a flash of disbelief as you read Aurora's words "I don't understand, but I forgive them" said within minutes of learning of her son's murder, so did I. And since then I have begun to reflect on forgiveness in a new way. And I have come to realize that there is a difference between grief and unforgiveness. Must unforgiveness, hatred, desire for revenge always cling to grief like bloodsucking leeches?

The answer is no. First of all, desire for justice is not the same as revenge. Revenge seeks personal pleasure in "making them pay." District attorney Susan Reed's desire for "stringing him up myself" approaches lust for personal revenge. Regret and anger at the crime are an echo of thirst for righteousness. But that alone does not begin to heal. Justice attempts to restore order. What is yet undone is the work of peace and healing, and that is the work of love. A man from our parish prayer group, with a wife and child, had a drinking problem. Worse, he got in his car and drove recklessly, smashing into a young man's car, killing him. While awaiting trial, contrite, he showed me the letter he was sending to the parents of the victim. The letter was brief but tearful. Crushed with grief, he even dared to ask their forgiveness. The parents stood near him to hear the sentence—eight years in prison. Justice of the court had done its duty. But God's work was not finished. Most often the family would nod with satisfaction that justice had been served, perhaps not as much as they would want. In this case, however, the parents came forward and offered their hand as a sign of forgiveness and reconciliation. They had been empowered by Christ's love.

Achieving Forgiveness— Leticia's Story

Not every story ends in immediate forgiveness. Leticia's story may help those of us who are still working at achieving forgiveness.

I thought I had become a professional at forgiveness. But this summer, I was faced with another grudge. Of all people, it was my older sister, whom I loved with all my heart. Jesus said we should forgive again and again. But this time, I did not think I could.

It began the day I had finally got the courage to tell my family that I was abused as a child. The abuser was my sister's husband! My sister was enraged. "You're crazy!" she yelled, her eyes flashing fire. "You want to tear our family apart!"

I could understand that she was angry because I had fingered her spouse, but she forgot that I was her sister. She was the one I had looked up to all my life. I wanted to be always with her, and I remember when I was small crying every time she left the house. Now, suddenly, she hated me. She wanted me out of her life.

I put the pain behind me as best I could and prayed that God would help her understand me and the pain I had already endured. Finally, my sister apologized to me and said she wanted to leave her husband, my abuser. My heart felt so free and I wanted to lift her above my head, shout for joy, and carry her on my back.

But it was too good to be true. When my abuser learned of my revelation, he attacked me. He punched me till blood streamed down my face. My sister merely watched from behind. The police came and asked for the account of the event from the witness—my sister. She looked at the officer and said those words that continue to ring in my head: "I do not remember." I had been betrayed by her once again.

That night, as I sat on the bed in the emergency room, she went back to him. She never called to see if I was okay. Shocked and bleary eyed, I did the incredible: I asked someone to call her to see if she was okay. Our sisterly bond somehow momentarily broke through my consciousness.

However, the pain of betrayal I had put behind me returned. I was betrayed twice. My parents wanted me to forgive her, but I could not. I tried to forget about her. I wanted to never see her again. Forgiveness was no longer an option. My days ahead were shadowed by a dark cloud. I could not find peace. Things that were important to me began to fall apart: school, work, and family.

One day in class, Father Montague spoke about forgiveness. I was reminded once again that Jesus forgave those who condemned him to death. I fought the words in my head. I went home that night after work and cried. I knew it would be the hardest thing to do, but Jesus wanted me to forgive my sister. With him I might even ask the Father to forgive her because she didn't know fully what she was doing or how deep was my hurt that she had caused.

The process is still ongoing but at least I now talk to her. Jesus never said that being a disciple was easy. I pray that soon, very soon, our relationship will improve so that I can not only tell her the depth of my hurt, but also that I forgive her. Hopefully, my forgiveness might awaken her sorrow for what she did. Through this process, I will be free because I have set her free. Soon, I hope.

10

PERSONAL STORIES OF MERCY

Confrontation— William's Story

Mercy is not for the weak. To give a coin to a beggar is no risk, but there are situations where mercy costs more than a coin. Jesus foresaw one of those cases when he said, "If another member of the church sins against you, go and point out the fault when the two of you are alone. If the member listens to you, you have regained that one" (Matt 18:15). Whether it is a member of our family or a member of a close group to which we belong, confronting a person is often a risk that we don't like to take. We would rather be loved by everyone, especially those close to us. If we confront that person, will we lose their love, their friendship?

Will they hereafter give us the iceberg treatment or never talk to us again?

Some prefer to ignore the fault or sweep it under the rug, or worse, complain to a third party, creating gossip—what Pope Francis has called terrorism. That may avoid conflict in the short run, but it is a wound that festers. Jesus, though, focuses on how confrontation can help us grow in our love for each other: "If the member listens to you, you have regained that one."

William Garza belonged to a fraternity, where he experienced the pain and the joy of such confrontation.

> I remember the day like it was yesterday. In my sophomore year, some friends and I decided to go to a party we had heard about. One of my very good friends and fraternity brother, John (I have changed his name), was going with us. We had some drinks before leaving for the party, but I did not, for I was the designated driver. By the time we got to the party, John was getting louder, which did not surprise me, because some people often do that when they drink. But shortly he began to get physical. So as a good friend, I told him that he should take it easy and maybe stop drinking. He saw this as an insult and said I was being rude and making him look bad. "No," I said, "you're making yourself look bad the way you're acting." He made a sarcastic remark and walked away.

As he began to drink more, I saw that the night was getting out of control. A former girlfriend of John's showed up with another fellow, and I immediately knew this was going to be a bad night. It wasn't long before John started talking with his ex-girlfriend and, when the guy wasn't looking, he made a pass at her. This led to a fight, but I finally got John home.

The next day I confronted John about the way he had acted and how it made him look in front of others. It seemed he understood. He said he would work on it. But a few weeks later I got a call from a close friend.

"Get over to this party quick. John is extremely drunk and is about to get into a fight with four different guys."

I got there just in the nick of time. I recognized one of the guys John was going to fight, so I told him there was no need to fight because I was going to take John home.

The next day my friends and I decided we needed to have a serious talk with John about the effect that alcohol was having on him.

This was very difficult for some of the guys to do.

"It looks like we're ganging up on him," they said.

"No," I said, "It's better that we gang up on him before he really gets ganged up on and beaten up for something he may say or do when he's drunk. We're not really ganging up on him. We're just trying to help out a friend in need."

Jesus said, "If your brother sins, go and tell him his fault between you and him alone….If he does not listen, take one or two others along with you, that every word may be confirmed."

My fraternity brothers and I did this for John, and we together "gained our brother."

Spiritual Richness— L. M. F.'s Story

One of the biggest obstacles to spiritual growth is becoming self-satisfied. This can even happen with very spiritual people. One semester, while teaching the Gospel of Mark, I was struck by this student's realization of self-satisfaction.

For the last six months I have been happy that my life is satisfactory. I have a loving family and loving friends that are like family. I have an awesome car and everything else. I go to Mass every Sunday, so I have felt that my faith is enough to get by—until we read the Gospel of Mark. A new light showed me that being satisfactory is not enough.

In Mark 10:17–22, a rich man comes up to Jesus and asks what he should do to gain eternal life.

"Keep the commandments," Jesus replies. Proudly the man tells Jesus, "I have stayed true to them since I was a little boy." He sounds like he is looking for something new, another challenge. Jesus gives it to him.

"Go, sell what you have and give to the poor and you will have treasure in heaven; then come, follow me." The man's face falls. He says nothing and walks away sad.

This man is spiritually rich. He is satisfied with the faith he has and will not risk more. When he hears the invitation, he retreats to the satisfaction of his life of wealth and comfort. He is not a great sinner. He keeps the commandments. He just loses the greatness he could become when the Lord invites him to a greater glory.

I am spiritually rich. I consider myself a good Catholic. I have gone to Catholic school my whole life, and I have also attended youth groups, taught CCD, staffed a Catholic camp twice and a conference once. I have been involved in youth ministry for eight years. I have helped many people. I am satisfied with the Catholic I have become. But should this satisfy me? Should I do more?

I am like this man in the Gospel of Mark. I feel I am called to something big, that God has a plan for me. But I hold on to what I have so much that I turn away from it. You see, not only am I satisfied with my faith, I am satisfied with my life the way it is and I am scared to give it up.

Lately, I have been praying to become empty, to give everything to God, and to become like the woman in Mark 12:42–44, who gave up everything she had to offer. She recognized that everything she had and everything she was belonged to God. She was truly "empty," and she longed to be filled with God and do anything for him.

Jesus saw in this woman what he himself was about to do. He was close to death. Like the woman who gave all, he is ready to give everything, his whole life to the Father. I would like to be a reminder to all of God—for people not to see me in my life but to see in me Jesus giving himself up for God.

Love of Self—Lena's Story

Mercy is just another form of love. And love starts with a love of self. What a joy to know someone who has grown in a real love of self so that they can let go of their own worries and give to others. Lena's story starts with worry and ends at the Sunday collection.

> Throughout my life I have stressed over the smallest things. Whether it is the way I look or how much money I need, I get snagged. In class, we talked about the Gospel reading:
>
> > *Do not worry about your life, what you will eat or what you will drink, or about your body, what you will wear....Can any of you by worrying add a single hour to your span of life?...Do not worry about tomorrow, for tomorrow will bring worries of its own. Today's trouble is enough for today.* (Matt 6:25–34; Luke 12:22–31)
>
> The Lord got my attention. Even when everything is going right, I can always find something to worry about. These verses really helped me step back and reevaluate my life and reactions.
>
> When it comes to physical fitness, I often find myself obsessing. I am constantly worrying about every meal and every calorie and how it might affect my body. I become more anxious with every bite, and soon I think of ways I can make up for a particularly bad meal. I am always concerned about how

I look. It's not so much about my clothes but more about my body itself.

In the gospel passage, I found Jesus saying that life is more than food. If God provides for the birds, he will provide for each of us. He isn't overly concerned with how we look on the outside but how we feel on the inside. The Bible encourages us to set aside worldly values, and to focus on the Lord and how he wants us to live our lives. I have decided that, while it is okay to be conscious of a healthy body, it is unhealthy to obsess over it and lose my focus on God.

My other daily anxiety is a never-ending concern with money. While I work two jobs, I am constantly worried that I don't make enough money. Even though I am still in school and living at home, I am always looking for ways to save so that I can become independent. I know being frugal with money is important, but over analyzing every purchase is tiring and stressful. Often, I don't want to purchase food to save a few dollars. It never really hit me until I saw how it was affecting my beliefs. Every Sunday as the offering baskets circulated through the congregation, I would feel this overwhelming fear. It reached the point where I would feel a physical pain as I placed a few dollars into the tray, knowing I should give more.

It wasn't until I started keeping a budget that things began to change. On Sunday, I would take out what I had budgeted from my last paycheck and place it in the offering tray with complete detachment. I didn't worry about what I could have purchased with that money or where exactly it was going. All that mattered was that I had learned to let go and let God work in my life. Soon, I noticed a change in my finances. More opportunities came to make some extra money. I knew it was God working in my life and providing me with blessings. Once I allowed myself to sow by opening my life to God, I began to reap.

Community—C. M.'s Story

The poet Dante, in his *Inferno*, describes the lowest point in hell not as the hottest furnace but as a block of ice. The condemned person is incased in it—a supreme isolation of his own making. Heaven, however, is a festive celebration of community, a joyful union with God, with the choirs of angels and all the redeemed. It is family. Of course, it will mean joyful union with those we were closest to on earth, but somehow there will be no more strangers. All are brothers and sisters.

The church is a rehearsal for heaven. It is an anticipation of heavenly community. Imperfect because it is a hospital for sinners, it nevertheless strives for *agape*, the divine love that binds, heals, and gives us a fore-taste of heavenly union. That is why, in God's plan, it is the way to salvation; choosing to swim alone in a roiling sea rather than sail home in a ship can be deadly.

Impressed with Matthew's teaching on church as community, C. M. told the following story:

> The community that Matthew portrays is inclusive, supportive, and giving. It is the heart of the church; without it, the church is just an institution. So, it is the responsibility of a Christian to be an active member of the community.
>
> As I was growing up, my parents participated eagerly in every event of our parish. Sundays after Mass we would get together with other members of the community to do some form of service. Some days, we would visit the aged and homebound; on other days, we would give things to the poor. Afterwards, we would usually get together at someone's house and, while the children played games, the grown-ups would talk, have coffee, and plan for other activities and works of charity. This was life-giving for all of us.
>
> My father was especially happy during those times. His eyes were always full of life and joy. However, after some time, for reasons I will never know, my father started to

change. He became more concerned with his job than with his family and the community. Often on Sundays my mother and I would have to respond to the question, "Where is he? He is not coming today?" Rather embarrassed, we would have to make up excuses for my father's absence. He never explained why he stopped coming and why he was alienating himself from us, his family, and our Christian community. The situation got worse until he left home and the church. He just disappeared.

That hit us hard. We became emotionally deflated. We didn't know why my father left family and community, and I grew bitterly angry at him for abandoning us. But we never stopped our Sunday routines. This was because the members of our church reached out to us. They were crucial in our survival. Thank God for community!

In a restaurant a few months later, I saw my father. He was alone. Against my feelings, for I was still bitterly angry and had not forgiven him, I went to say "hello." As I got closer, I realized that the man I saw was not my father. He looked tired, unshaven, with black circles around his eyes, and a horrible look of sadness and grief on his face. Relieved that I had made a mistake and wasn't going to have to face my father after all, I turned to walk away. But just then he called my name. It was my father! I was shocked. I sat down with him and—incredibly—my hate melted into compassion.

We had a long talk. He explained to me that, after he left, an immense guilt and loneliness invaded his soul. He had stopped going to church because he was so embarrassed for what he had done to us, and he couldn't even make sense of why he had left—even now, the reasons are not clear to any of us. It doesn't matter. I couldn't find any intelligent words to comfort him. I just invited him to come to Mass next Sunday. He did, and we all welcomed him with open arms.

Jesus told the parable of the prodigal son. We have our story of the prodigal father. Our community helped my father get his feet back on the ground and set his priorities straight. The prodigal son had foolish reasons for leaving home, but he returned repentant to his father's arms; our father had unknown reasons for leaving our loving and outgoing community, but he found open arms on his return. Back in the community that loved him, my father was home again.

11

THE MYSTERY OF INEQUALITY

On the ranch, the nightly starlit dome and the daily wonders of nature were not the only teachers of life. Another taught us of the grim reality of our past that lay on the ground beneath our feet. As I walked along a path cleared for a powerline near the river, amid a cluster of common sherds, my eyes caught a chiseled flint, and within a second, I held a perfectly worked arrowhead in the palm of my hand.

If only it could speak! How long ago did some hunter-warrior chip you from anonymous flint to make you into a weapon? Was it as late as the nineteenth century, when the first settlers feared you as they came to draw water at our spring? Or was it twelve thousand years earlier, when you pierced your first American buffalo, enabling the tribe to eat? Arrowheads guard their secrets.

Atsila and the Arrowhead

Even so, I press my questions. What is the name of the brave who last fired you? As I imagine him in moccasins creeping past me, I decide to call him *Atsila*, Cherokee for "fire," that element that can consume or comfort, as needed. Most theologies would agree that God is similar. And Atsila, if you are human, you are like that too. You may have already killed a settler who encroached on your hunting land, but you have surely already embraced your children with love. Doing one for the sake of the other, you know hate, but you also know love.

A feeling of kinship, even of brotherhood, with Atsila came over me. I have also known hate and love. Not only that, my eldest brother, Frank, often repeated our grandfather's claim that he spent much of his childhood on an Indian reservation, having been born to a Cherokee mother. Frank's daughters even today attest to the family tradition, though ancestry research has yet to confirm it. Trusting the family tradition, I claim that one-eighth of my blood is Cherokee. That's why I chose to give my imaginary person a Cherokee name, though the arrowhead may have just as likely been used by a Comanche. That's why the history of the Indigenous Americans being herded like sheep from their homeland to an Oklahoma reservation on the deadly Trail of Tears is part of our family history, and mine.

Atsila, there are many things that you could teach me—about bravery, about stealth in hunting, and about loyalty to your family and tribe. But when I think of the one thing you are missing, I am filled with sadness and compassion. You don't know Jesus.

Meeting the God of Mercy

And here is where you cease to be imaginary. You stand for the billions of human beings, past and present, who, through no fault of their own, have never encountered him as their Lord and Savior. Nor have they experienced the divine love, joy, and peace given by the Holy Spirit. Is there any chance for you to meet the God of Mercy? Like a train slowing to meet its destination, this narrative is winding down to the same puzzle with which it started: the mystery of inequality. And the answer is the same: we are the receivers, not the Giver nor the judge, of the gift. But whatever the gift, we are responsible for its use. Those who are gifted with faith are expected to share it. But expected by whom? By the Giver, whose gifts are given to be shared.

But even if today all the world's believers would receive a tsunami of grace to evangelize the living, they would not be able to reach everyone. And what of the billions of men, women, and children whose skeletons litter the earth from the beginning and who have never heard of God's plan in Christ for humankind? Today, most theologians consider the possibility of "baptism of desire" to suffice for those men, women, and children. In other words, they have a notion of the Supreme Being's provision for the grace of repentance in the light of God "who desires everyone to be saved and to come to the knowledge of the truth" (1 Tim 2:4). And John the Evangelist tells us that the light of God is offered to everyone and that those "who do what is true come to the light, so that it may be clearly seen that their deeds have been done in God" (John 3:21).

The Second Vatican Council comments, "Since Christ died for all men, and since the ultimate vocation of man is in fact one, and divine, we ought to believe that the Holy Spirit in a manner known only to God offers to every man the possibility of being associated with this paschal mystery" (*Gaudium et Spes* 22). However ultimate and ambiguous, there is a chance, therefore, for them to grab the lifesaver of God's mercy. Given our awareness of our nature's inclination to sin and selfishness and the vast numbers, past and present, who have no sense of an eternal responsibility, we tend to think it rare that the uninstructed would even see the lifesaver of Mercy floating on the sea of terror at death. Still, the mystery is God's, and not ours, to resolve. But the urgency of evangelizing spurs us on because introducing the uninstructed to Jesus, the Holy Spirit, and the church gives the best chance of leading them to eternal life.

In the history of the Southwest, there were two main methods of "pacifying" the Indigenous Americans. One method was to herd people like sheep from their tepees and hunting lands to reservations, the

"Trail of Tears" approach. The Cherokees alone lost four thousand members on the three-month journey.

The other method was undertaken by troops of robed friars who set up missions where communities of Indigenous Americans could be fed, educated in language and other skills, and protected from marauding bands—and taught the Christian faith. Not all the friars' communities escaped the marauders. On April 16, 1758, some two thousand Comanches and allies destroyed the Mission Santa Cruz de San Sabá in central Texas, killing two friars and eight Apache under their care. When my father built our rock home on the ranch in 1939, he memorialized the mission by incorporating some of its ruins in the walls. The method of the missions was more respectful of personal freedom and planted the seed of a new Hispanic-Native American people. I have been blessed by serving these people in a majority-minority university (Saint Mary's, San Antonio) for forty years, retiring just in time to finish this book. The soil that one day will bury my body may be six feet deep, but it will never equal the gratitude that covers me for so many years of grace.

12

YOUR STORY

Personal Reflection

This chapter is for your own personal reflection and/or journal writing. The following questions are presented to help you get started. They may also be useful for a group discussion.

1. Did reading these stories of God's mercy lead you to ponder your own experiences of giving or receiving mercy?

2. Do you see your life as a gift of God's mercy?

3. Can you remember an event in your life in which you received mercy?

4. Do you remember a time when you extended mercy to someone?

5. How do you deal with the difference in other people's gifts and opportunities in life?

6. Which of the personal stories resonated most deeply with your own experience?

7. What role has prayer had in your experiences of mercy?

8. How have you experienced forgiveness in your life?

9. Has your life been a blessing or a burden? Why?